BUILDING BETTER
PUBLIC SERVICES

A Guide for Practitioners

TONY DEAN

 FriesenPress

Suite 300 - 990 Fort St
Victoria, BC, Canada, V8V 3K2
www.friesenpress.com

ISBN
978-1-4602-6972-5 (Hardcover)
978-1-4602-6973-2 (Paperback)
978-1-4602-6974-9 (eBook)

1. Political Science, Public Policy

Distributed to the trade by The Ingram Book Company

TABLE OF CONTENTS

Chapter 5

Chapter 6

PREFACE

As a fifteen-year-old school leaver, I'm one of those beneficiaries of second and third chances. After a series of unskilled jobs in my home town of Birmingham in the UK, I apprenticed as a millwright at the Dunlop Tire Factory not far from my parents' home. Millwrighting is the craft of installing or repairing industrial machinery. In my case it involved repairing tire-making equipment. As it turned out, I was not a very good millwright. I had no difficulty taking machinery apart but was seriously challenged in the art of reassembly, which is a fairly big part of the job.

My involvement in an engineering workers' union led me to a placement as a mature student in a trade union sponsored college in a leafy neighbourhood near Birmingham University. I was ready for this second chance at an education and it was where my lifelong interest in labour-management relations took root. A university degree followed, then a spur of the moment move to Hamilton, Ontario for a master's degree in sociology. Beyond the great fortune of studying in Canada, I met my wife and made my home here. After several years working as a union representative, I was lucky enough to land a job as a policy advisor at Ontario's Ministry of Labour.

Some jobs provide for an elixir of past experience and current interests, which leads to unexpected places and this was certainly the case for me. I loved that job. I brought some practical expertise to it but was given a far greater opportunity to learn the practice and art of public administration and public policy-making. I was privileged to learn from terrific public services leaders who each in their own way took a chance on me, and also threw me into the deep end for challenging sink-or-swim learning experiences. In working for three very different political administrations I also learned about the complex interplay between politics and public administration.

My eventual move into the job of Cabinet Secretary and head of Canada's largest provincial public service says a lot more about the culture, leadership and staff of Ontario's Public Service than it does about me. I was supported at every step. I worked with impressive and committed political leaders who invariably wanted the best advice from the public service and expected its best professional support. In my view, political leaders received that support and they still do. Although I recall Dalton McGuinty, Ontario's Premier from 2003 to 2013, for whom I have great respect, saying wryly that I had "executed" some of his best ideas.

I have had the rare opportunity to see the work of a large and complex organization both from the crow's nest and on the ground: with firefighting crews in northern Ontario; health and safety inspectors dealing with the aftermath of workplace injury and death; policy managers developing strategies to keep vulnerable children safe from harm; and front-line public health professionals responding to the SARS crisis in Toronto in 2003. I am a supporter of public services and have great respect for public servants and their leaders. They hold a significant responsibility in their hands and they take that responsibility very seriously. This is virtuous and important work. I want our public services to work well for citizens and especially for those who must rely on those services.

Through a foreign assignment in London in 2008 and research projects that followed, I had the opportunity to study aggressive public service reforms in the United Kingdom and to compare these with the experience of Canada and other western countries. While there are obvious differences in culture and politics, it occurred to me that many governments were experiencing similar pressures from global economic changes, citizens' expectations of government, and the myriad social and technical impacts of digitization.

I now have the further privilege of teaching graduate students at the School of Public Policy and Governance at the University of Toronto, where I am very slowly crossing the bridge from practice to academia, without an expectation that I will reach the other side. The School attracts bright and ambitious students, and in one seminar I was talking about the relationship between policy, delivery, and funding silos in the public sector when a student asked me, "is this stuff written down anywhere." It was a good question, and this book is its outcome. It has been tailored for students of public policy and public administration, and for public service practitioners and leaders.

The governing idea of the book is this: If public service organizations do a small number of things really well they can develop into great organizations and accomplish great things. We should expect no less.

ACKNOWLEDGEMENTS

In writing this book, I'm indebted to public service managers and leaders who took a chance on me early in my career; to public service reformers in Canada and the UK; and, to those who have generously reviewed manuscripts.

I was thrown into deep end opportunities by my first Deputy Minister, Glenn Thompson, and in turn by others including George Thomson, Jim Thomas, Tim Millard and Cynthia Morton. They each took a chance on me and paved my way to an eventual appointment as Deputy Minister of Labour. Former Ontario Cabinet Secretary Rita Burak brought me into the environment of the Cabinet Office and readied me as a potential successor. Alex Himelfarb and Kevin Lynch were my federal counterparts during my time as Cabinet Secretary and gave me important insights into the complexities of federalism and intergovernmental relationships. Working with Alex Himelfarb in the heat of inter-governmental negotiations on the ten-year health accord in 2004 was a highlight of my professional career.

I've had the privilege of working for the three major political parties in Ontario, and to work closely with four Ontario premiers: Mike Harris, Ernie Eves, Dalton McGuinty and Kathleen Wynne. Each offered an important window on the rich relationship between politics and public administration, and they all respected the public service and were prepared to listen to its advice. Our advice was not always determinative but it was invariably heard. This reinforced my strong belief in the important role of public servants in the effective functioning of democratic governments.

Research on public service reform in the United Kingdom in 2008 and 2009 led to renewed contact with Sir Michael Barber and informative talks with Ray Shostak who succeeded Michael as head of the UK Prime Minister's

Delivery Unit (PMDU). I also learned much from Guy Lodge, Gillian Licari at Canada's High Commission in London, and the impressive team of researchers at The Institute for Government.

In 2009, Mark Stabile, the inaugural Director at the School of Public Policy at the University of Toronto, invited me to teach a graduate course at the school. This opportunity enriched my professional life and started the momentum towards this book. Graduate students in my class suggested the need for a book of this kind and in 2014, forty-four students were kind enough to test run some key chapters as course content.

Two anonymous peer reviewers assigned by a Canadian academic press provided extensive comments on an early manuscript resulting in substantial revisions and a much stronger product which was helped considerably by Jennifer Simpson's thorough editing job. Marie Boutilier, Patrice Dutil, Jennifer Gold, Josh Hjartarson, Alex Himelfarb, Mark Jarvis, Bob Rae and Ray Shostak have also been generous in reviewing and commenting on subsequent drafts.

The Institute of Public Administration of Canada (IPAC) is Canada's foremost association of public servants, academics, and others interested in public administration. It has been a major force in exporting successful Canadian public sector expertise around the world. IPAC has supported my work in the past and has been generous in supporting the publication of this book. I want to thank long-term colleague Ann Masson, IPAC's Director of Domestic and International Programs, and Andrea Migone, Director of Research and Outreach, for reading the manuscript and encouraging me to finish this work. I'm also grateful to the Ottawa-based Forum of Federations and to Leslie Seidle for supporting research cited in this book.

I must also recognize the terrific professional team at Friesen Press who have done a marvellous job in editing and designing the book. I could not have been better served or supported from beginning to end.

Meeting my spouse Marie Boutilier in 1978 turned a one-year overseas master's program into a lifelong commitment. I've been alongside the right person, in the right country, ever since. Marie is an accomplished researcher and writer and I'm her partner in a small consulting company. We have teamed up for several overseas research projects, some of which are represented in this book. We meet comfortably in the middle of the bridge between theory and practice. I count my blessings every day.

My son David also reviewed the manuscript and encouraged me to finish this project. We are great friends and spend our best times together at our camp on the Montreal River in northern Ontario where ideas in this book have been discussed at length.

CHAPTER 1
INTRODUCTION

Canada's public services are under threat. Years of economic uncertainty, declining revenues and burgeoning demands from service users has resulted in endemic fiscal deficits and constraints in many areas of public service. This has prompted fresh demands for smaller, leaner government and more efficient modes of public service delivery. There are parallel pressures from the demographically-driven expectations of an aging population, and many other clients of public services with multiple needs. Further, political leaders have become fearful about raising taxes. Pledges to hold the line or reduce taxes have become commonplace in election platforms. Alex Himelfarb (2013) noted that a steady menu of tax cuts has drained revenues without delivering on the promised growth to offset or exceed those cuts. Politicians also face a growing "trust deficit" in their relationship with citizens, turnouts in general elections are falling steadily, and governments' stakeholders are feeling disenfranchised from decision-making processes. There are concerns about the efficacy of our democratic institutions. Collectively, these changes and pressures are raising some fundamental questions about the role of the state and the nature and delivery of public services in Canada and elsewhere.

In the face of these pressures, conservatives argue that smaller government is better, often leading to arbitrary efforts to cut spending without regard to improving public services. On the other hand, the political left and, in some cases, the labour movement's response has focused on raising revenues in order to protect the status quo in public services, which in some cases does not work very well. In between, there are a number of policy and political choices about an alternative path, many of which have been set out in both government-commissioned reports (Drummond 2012), and by policy research organizations (Gold, Mendelsohn and Hjartarson 2011; Partnership for Public Service 2011). These approaches, which focus on making public services more efficient and effective, are important for people who need public services; for the political leaders who are held to account for the performance of government as a whole; and, for public servants and their partners in other sectors who work hard to serve both citizens and the elected government of the day.

Public service leaders around the world have been responding to these challenges and we have learned a great deal from their experimentation and innovation. Canada has been a global leader in many areas of public service reform, including taking policy-based approaches to deficit reduction, integrating front counter and online services, and experimenting with public-private partnerships. Canadian efforts to measure citizen satisfaction with service delivery have demonstrated that service users' experience of government services influences their perception of government and the public sector generally (Institute for Citizen-Centred Service 2005).

New and transformational approaches to public service can result in the provision of better services at less cost.

Directionally, public services are becoming more citizen-focused; they are integrating previously fragmented services and are achieving significant results in hard to influence sectors such as health care (Fenn 2006) and education (Fullan 2006). We are also seeing early benefits from digitization and online service delivery and in the development of integrated case management systems (Dean and Boutilier 2012). Breakthroughs by delivery experts such as Michael Barber (2007) in the United Kingdom have demonstrated what it takes to successfully implement large and complex policy initiatives and we have benefitted from learning about problem solving in public sector delivery and the world of risk management and regulation from thought leaders like Malcolm Sparrow (2008). But the pressures for change are accelerating and public services have a long way to go in both meeting citizens' expectations and in demonstrating the ongoing relevance and virtues of public services and the public sector. New and transformational approaches to public service delivery can result in the provision of better services at less cost. At the same time, it is possible to create more inclusive relationships with citizens and communities by asking about their priorities and involving them in the design of programs and services. This will require a deeper and accelerated approach to reshaping public services to better meet the needs of service users.

Public service organizations are filled with creative and energetic people who work hard to respond to the needs and aspirations of citizens who depend on government services. The vast majority of public servants are both passionate and proud. They go to work every day inspired by their ability and responsibility to make a difference in the lives of those they serve. And they do this in thousands of ways every day, year in and year out. Like many public sector organizations – especially those with Westminster systems of government – Canada's public services are traditional in many respects, but their public servants innovate in big and small ways. There is no "one-size-fits-all" prescription for success because every organization is different, with its own history, culture, and stage of development. Canadian public servants are constantly looking throughout Canada and around the world for new approaches and innovations in policy-making and service delivery. At the same time, important pockets of innovation and greatness are present in most organizations and we can often learn best from close-to-home transformation efforts inside our own organizations. These are often not sufficiently captured, shared, and applauded.

A MAP OF THE BOOK

This book describes an important moment of change in public service organizations. It focuses on recent changes in the design and implementation of public policy and the delivery of public services, drawing on case studies, predominantly from Canada, and in a more limited way, from the United Kingdom. The case studies, and examples from my own experience and reflections on how governments work, include the design and implementation of political priorities, improvements to over-the-counter and online transactional services (such as the issuance of driver's licences and health cards), and the design and delivery of more complex human services. The book explores interconnections and synergies between emerging forms of public engagement, policy and program design and implementation, public service leadership and modern human resource strategies. Together with my own "reflective practice" (Schön 1983), this provides a basis from which lessons for governments, public service leaders, and practitioners are drawn. It seems to me that this is seldom done elsewhere.

I examine emerging ways in which governments are responding in a period of significant upheaval. The starting point is an examination of the siloed architecture of Westminster models of government and I then review in some detail the move towards more open and integrated policy-making and service delivery. Recent trends in the integration of transactional front counter services are examined as well as the more complex world of human service delivery. The book also looks at recent and more transformative approaches to deficit reduction with a particular emphasis on Canada, but drawing from other jurisdictions where necessary. I conclude with a chapter on the rarely discussed subject of leadership practice in the public sector, including the importance of human resource leadership.

I propose that if governments and public service leaders can find ways to accelerate these practices, and understand the synergies between them, good organizations can become great organizations and accomplish great things. Key success factors in all of these areas of reform are strong public service and political leadership, and high-level capacity for human resources (HR) strategy. Too much lip service is still paid to the work of HR leaders and practitioners, which has yet to achieve parity with the esteem accorded to policy-makers. Capacity gaps in public service organizations will be mentioned frequently in the chapters that follow, especially with respect to emerging skill requirements for policy-making, governance, risk management and network management.

This book is written for political and public service leaders, managers, and staff involved in policy development and direct service delivery, as well as teachers, journalists, and students of public policy and public administration. The book is not intended as a scholarly text; rather, it is a descriptive account of an important moment of change in the way public services are organized and delivered, from a practitioner's point of view. Lessons for governments, practitioners and students of public policy and public administration are provided at the end of each chapter. For those interested in the theory of public administration this work is best understood in the context of the transition from the "New Public Management" (Hood 1991; Aucoin 1990), towards the "New Public Governance" (Osborne 2010).

Chapter 2 looks in more detail at the significant fiscal, demographic and technologically-driven developments that are combining to influence change in government and in public sector organizations. Chapter 3 describes the architecture of Westminster models of government. The nature of ministry-based silos is discussed, together with the implications of jurisdictional, professional, and funding silos.

Subsequent chapters address public sector responses to the various pressures on governments and focus on sustaining or improving important public services at a lower cost.

Chapter 4 looks at efforts to integrate policy-making across government and outside of it through the development of more collaborative policy-making and program design with government stakeholders, citizens and service users; it also considers the policy-delivery continuum, looking at the UK's experience with breakthroughs in the implementation of large cross-ministry priorities and later modifications made in Canada.

Chapter 5 provides an overview of government approaches to tackling fiscal deficits. Drawing on recent studies from Canada and the UK, this chapter distinguishes between common, across-the-board approaches to budget cuts with arbitrary budget and staff reduction targets, and more transformational approaches which seek to prioritize, sustain and improve the public services that matter most to citizens.

Chapter 6 discusses the somewhat controversial area of Alternative Service Delivery (ASD), another area in which Canada has been an international leader. This field incorporates Public-Private Partnerships (P3s) on infrastructure projects, as well as the innovative development of Delegated Administrative Authorities (DAAs) in the province of Ontario.

Chapter 7 focuses on areas in which governments are working across organizational boundaries and removing duplication in the transition to more "joined-up" service delivery. I examine Canadian experience as a global pacesetter in the integration of front-counter and online service delivery. This chapter also reviews efforts to develop integrated approaches to the provision of services in the high-cost and complex areas of health, social services and justice services. Both UK and Canadian examples are discussed. In both of these areas of delivery it is becoming evident that digital modes of service delivery and information sharing are on the ascendancy and will become an increasingly important enabler of public service reform.

Chapter 8 discusses the critical role of leadership in the public sector, particularly in the context of leading change in traditional and hierarchical organizations. Strong leadership is both undervalued and underplayed in public sector organizations and a case is made for a necessary shift to more activist public sector leadership. Deference to elected political leaders in matters of policy, governance and decision-making architecture is important. But alongside this, organizational leadership and building capacity for better planning, policy development and delivery lies in the hands of public service leaders – as does bringing out the very best from public servants. This chapter also discusses the importance of a focused strategic approach to human resources management which, it is argued, must be elevated and given parity of esteem with policy development.

Chapter 9 consolidates advice for government and practitioners, drawn from the case studies and also sets out my views on the principal elements and enablers of public service reform.

CHAPTER 2

PRESSURES FOR CHANGE AND GOVERNMENT RESPONSES

For the past three decades, governments have responded to demands for greater efficiency, effectiveness, and customer responsiveness by reforming and modernizing public services. This chapter reviews the pressures that have given rise to reform efforts, with reference where appropriate to theories of public administration and management.

PRESSURES DRIVING PUBLIC SERVICES REFORM

There are several major drivers of public service reforms. These include changing demographics, the burgeoning expectations of highly educated and well-resourced citizens, budget pressures, and a growing sense that in view of the scale of the public sector in advanced economies, efforts should be made to ensure that public services are operating efficiently

In 2008, the sub-prime mortgage crisis, which had its most direct impact in the United States, the United Kingdom, and Ireland, provoked a serious economic recession. This caused millions of people to lose their homes and left many more millions of homeowners owing more to mortgage lenders than their properties were worth. The damage caused by the resulting debt crisis continues to rattle global markets. Hundreds of billions of dollars of taxpayer's money has been spent by governments in North America and Europe to stabilize banks, and other financial institutions, and on stimulus measures to prevent an economic free fall. In short, the world learned that the debt crisis is not just about over-leveraged homeowners. Most countries in the developed world have been living way beyond their means. From 2009 to 2011, Europe's major economies, with the exception of Germany, melted down. We remain in the midst of a serious global economic slowdown with no signs of an early recovery. Declining revenues from a slumping economy, public money spent on private sector bailouts, and efforts to reactivate the economy have resulted in ballooning government deficits. Canadian and U.S. governments were already spending more money than they raised through taxation, and their debt crises have recently intensified.

Governments around the globe are shrinking public service staff levels, and many are reconfiguring compensation and pension schemes to provide greater comparability with those in the private sector. Hundreds of thousands of jobs have been lost in North America. U.S. states with balanced budget laws are cutting services, shedding staff, and implementing "furloughs" in which services – including schools – are experiencing temporary shutdowns. The 2012-13 federal budget in Canada cut $5.2 billion in spending and 19,000 jobs (or 4.8 per cent of the workforce) as a result of a Strategic Operating Review. The 2015-16 federal budget increases projected job losses to 50,000. Similar programs are under way in Ontario, the country's most populous province. Ontario's 2015-16 budget outlines a plan to eliminate the province's $10.9 billion deficit by 2017-2018 and 1,500 public service jobs have been eliminated for a total of 5,000 since 2008 (7.5 per cent of the workforce).

Spending on public services has been constrained for a number of years and serious efforts to reform public services have been accelerating since the mid-1970s. In Canadian provinces, new spending has been almost exclusively focused on political priorities such as health care where, until very recently, over six per cent increases in annual spending has far exceeded revenue growth. Federal spending has been directed at national political priorities such as defence and justice. Increases in these expensive areas continue to draw resources away from other departments, causing them to wrestle with flatlined budgets and successive program reviews. Piled on top of this are huge demographically-driven demands for government programs. Canada and the UK share a similar demographic profile, and both countries will see an avalanche of aging citizens with their associated health and community care demands over the next decade or so. Emergency rooms in both countries are already overcrowded, and too many high-cost critical care beds in hospitals are occupied by patients who just need community or supported home-based care.

A 2010 Ontario Hospital Association study reported that one per cent of the Ontario population accounts for 49 per cent of combined hospital and home care costs, while five per cent of the population accounts for 84 per cent of combined hospital and home care costs and this is well before the province and Canada as a whole will reach the crest of its demographic wave (Ontario Hospital Association 2010). In addition, the Ontario government's health expenditure has doubled from $21.6 billion in 1999 to a forecast $50 billion (Sousa 2014). Preventable chronic diseases and the high-cost drugs needed to treat them (the cost of which is rising at a rate of 9.2 per cent annually) are swallowing up an increasing share of health care budgets. These pressures will intensify in the coming years.

The democratization of information brought about by the Internet and the proliferation of 24-hour news outlets has changed the playing field for government.

These fiscal and demographic pressures are paralleled, paradoxically, by deep political fears about raising tax revenues. Indeed, there is an impetus to reduce taxes in an effort to stimulate both investment and spending, especially among conservative politicians. At the same time, politicians facing a growing democratic or "trust" deficit in their relationship with citizens. Governments have lost their hegemony in both communications and policy development. The democratization of information brought about by the Internet and the proliferation of 24-hour news outlets has changed the playing field for government.

Taken together, these changes are placing unprecedented pressures on public services. In turn, this is raising some fundamental questions about the role of the state, existing service levels, and modes of delivering publicly funded services. Governments and public sector leaders face the dual challenge of providing critical public services with less money while managing the rising expectations of citizens for more and better services.

In view of the large fiscal deficits facing many jurisdictions, it is unlikely that balanced budgets can be achieved solely through spending reductions (OECD 2012).

At the same time, transforming public services to make them more efficient and citizen friendly is something that should be pursued even when revenues are rising in the absence of a fiscal crisis (Drummond 2012). It is simply the right thing to do. Hjartarson et al. (2014) have pointed out that government comprises a major component of the economy. They note that Canadian public sector spending accounts for 20 per cent of Gross Domestic Product (GDP) and the public sector accounts for 25 per cent of total employment, making the public sector larger than Canada's manufacturing and financial services sectors combined. There is considerable room for efficiencies.

This is not a situation in which public service leaders can sit tight and wait for political leaders to save the day with large tax increases. New revenues may be part of the solution, to the extent that there is public tolerance for this, but a significant responsibility for sustaining and renewing public services lies in the hands of public servants and their leaders. There are three reasons for this:

1. Public servants have the knowledge and expertise to get this job done;
2. They have a professional responsibility to do it; and,
3. Good public administration makes for good politics.

If public servants chart a sensible and credible course, it has every chance of finding political support that is likely to be sustained across different political administrations. This is precisely what happened when the UK's Ministry of Justice embarked on its "Transforming Justice" program in 2009 (Institute for Government 2011). The program survived the change in government in 2010, as well as cabinet shuffles. Efforts to consolidate and integrate previously fragmented public services, such as with Service Canada and Australia's Centrelink, have also been sustained across different political administrations (Dean 2011).

This is a moment of crisis for public services. The challenges are becoming more complex and senior public servants must step forward to build bridges to a new generation of public services. How are they going to do this? The answer lies, at least partially, in deepening and accelerating a public service reform journey that has been under way in many jurisdictions for a number of years. So at the outset, it is important not to lose sight of how far public service reforms have evolved over the past three decades.

GOVERNMENT RESPONSES: THE EVOLUTION OF PUBLIC ADMINISTRATION AND PUBLIC MANAGEMENT

There has been an ongoing evolution in modern public administration and management in North America over the past 150 years, and particularly since the growth and emerging influence of a professional public service (Lynn 2006). This period has seen several major phases of public administration, from the rule-based and bureaucratic "traditional public administration" (Lynn 2006), through the transfer of "scientific" approaches to management from the private to the public sector (Gulick 1937.) The rise of the "New Public Management" in the mid-1970s concretized what had been a growing interest in managerialism in the public sector. It also reflected long-standing concerns about the influence of public servants on their political masters and a neo-liberal view of government and public services (Aucoin 1990, 126; Hood 1991).

The New Public Management was popularized by Osborne and Gaebler in their bestselling book *Reinventing Government* (Osborne and Gaebler 1993). Drawing on contemporary examples of innovation in management, Osborne and Gaebler captured the imaginations of political leaders in North America and Europe with their notions of mission-driven government, "steering not rowing", and outcomes-focused, competitive, and customer-driven government. For many years, this book was seen by critics as a rallying cry for a neo-liberal approach to public service delivery. In retrospect, the book lays out a fairly sensible approach to rethinking the way we do business in government. A case in point is Osborne and Gaebler's call for more rigor in measuring what government does and the results it gets for the money invested in public services ("what gets measured gets done"). This is an area in which governments continue to struggle. Billions of dollars are spent in the highest cost areas of government service delivery – health, education,

> **Billions of dollars are spent in the highest cost areas of government service delivery – health, education, justice, social and children's services – and yet we have very little idea of the results being achieved for those investments.**

justice, social and children's services – and yet we have very little idea of the results being achieved for those investments. To some degree, many of those original principles set out in 1993 can be found in current public service reform plans.

More recently, the application of network theory (Castells 1996), horizontal management (Lindquist 2012), and the broader concept of the New Public Governance (Osborne 2010) have been considered more relevant in responding to disaggregated government structures, the growth of complex service delivery partnerships, and growing citizen and stakeholder expectations for greater involvement in policy-making, program design, and decision-making (Osborne 2010).

In practice, these major phases of public administration and management overlap, and it is not unusual to find elements of traditional administration, new public management, and networked management and delivery coexisting within the same organization (Pollitt and Bouckaert 2011, 12).

Almost universally, contemporary public service reform plans tend to focus on modernizing administrative systems and approaches to policy making and service delivery, with an underlying objective of improving quality and efficiency (U.K. Cabinet Office 2009; Drummond 2012).

These major trends in reform include:

- Integrating government operations and services within and across government departments;

- An emphasis on citizen-centred services designed around the needs of service users. A shift in culture towards a more customer-driven government has taken on significant importance and it is common to see this as one of the centrepiece initiatives in public sector reform plans (U.K. Cabinet Office 2009);

- The use of new technologies and digitization to reduce transaction costs and improve service delivery to citizens (e.g., online services, customer relationship management and client case management, as in the case of ServiceOntario and Service B.C.);

- Developing alternative approaches to delivering on major political priorities (as well as service delivery) that involve a range of partners in the public, private, and social sectors (e.g., the Community Budgets projects in the UK discussed in Chapter 8); and,

- Designing and evaluating services on the basis of measurable outcomes rather than inputs/outputs (Galley, Gold and Johal 2013).

The drivers of reform in the public sector are readily identifiable as are some of the major approaches to reform, which tend to be fairly common across jurisdictional boundaries. In the balance of the book we explore reform initiatives in greater detail and draw out advice for leaders and practitioners. But first, in view of widespread reform efforts over several decades it would fair to ask why more progress has not been made. There are many reasons for this including political risk aversion, turf protection at senior levels of the public service, uncertainty about where leadership responsibility lies, and the architecture of government. While we will touch on each of these areas, the challenge of architecture is discussed in the next chapter.

CHAPTER 3
THE ARCHITECTURE OF GOVERNMENT

PHYSICAL ARCHITECTURE: SEARCHING FOR GOVERNMENT

Many of the architectural features of the organization of government have remained unchanged for decades. In 1965, this was captured well in popular literature in the opening passage of Sjowall and Wahloo's first Martin Beck mystery *Roseanna,* which describes the inter-departmental fiasco associated with finding the machinery necessary to dredge a canal (Sjowall and Wahloo, 2008). It is still very much in evidence today.

Anyone who has worked in government – ministers, senior public servants, staff, and even student interns – recognizes its complex and compartmentalized organizational structure. As government grew following the Second World War, the number of ministries (or "departments" as they are called federally in Canada, the USA and the UK) grew in turn, each with its own minister and public service staff, payroll, purchasing, HR, and later, information technology (IT) offices. Each ministry also maintained its own capacity for research, policy development, and communications. Ministries also operated their own front counters to provide services to citizens – so, for example, losing a purse or wallet meant several trips around town to different front counters in separate offices. In federal jurisdictions such as Australia and Canada, these offices could be run without any coordination by up to three levels of government. While this is changing, many areas of government continue to be siloed. For example, ministries with a regulatory mandate still maintain their own separate cadre of inspectors, legal departments, and enforcement staff, and are disinclined to encroach on one another's turf. There is comfort in knowing where the boundaries are and in playing close to home.

Siloed organizational structures are a significant impediment to improving the quality and efficiency of public services.

Ministries often operate like separate and independent governments. They develop specific cultures and are focused on their own policy issues and stakeholders. When this author joined the public service in 1989, ministry turf was explicitly and often fiercely defended, and in many cases this still goes on in governments all over the world. As a case in point, in a 2011 hearing of the UK parliament's Select Committee on Public Administration, which was examining the splitting of the Cabinet Secretary's position into two jobs, the UK's departmental structure was described by a former Cabinet Secretary as operating more like a "federation" of relatively independent entities as opposed to being part of a single corporation (House of Commons, 2011).

Siloed organizational structures are a significant impediment to improving the quality and efficiency of public services. We regularly read about social assistance clients "falling through the cracks" between a dozen or more social service agencies they are in contact with across the health, social care and justice sectors. Without fail, whenever something goes seriously wrong and government actions or preparedness are put under a microscope, a story emerges of disconnected departments not working together or not sharing critical data. There are big examples. Reports on the performance of government leading up to or following 9/11, Hurricane Katrina, SARS, the Walkerton water crisis, and the flubbed reconstruction of post-earthquake Haiti all point to the vulnerabilities caused by siloed organizations and siloed thinking. This has to change.

New programs and services are continually implemented to deliver on election campaign commitments, in response to emerging issues, or because there is a public policy imperative. The problem is that new programs have often been layered over existing programs like layers of paint – often without a full assessment of pre-existing services, and hence potential synergies, in the same field of policy or service delivery. Eggers and O'Leary (2009) illustrate this well with the story of a failed public housing complex in St Louis, which was literally dynamited to rubble, in contrast to the "perma-tweaking" of existing programs that is so prevalent in the public sector.

Each generation of political and public service leaders inherits this legacy architecture, which in view of its size and complexity appears immutable. Since each ministry maintains close relationships with its respective stakeholder communities, there would be a political price to pay if, for example, farmers or the environmental community lost their most popular programs. This has especially been the case in Westminster models of government, where separate departments or ministries led by political ministers have traditionally operated in relative isolation as mini-governments fighting for their turf.

SILOED AND DUPLICATED SERVICES

Siloed structures are usually accompanied by duplicated functions and services, both within and between departments and governments. This occurs at almost every level and affects both professional and transactional services. For example, in each department, professional internal services are provided to the political administration and senior public service leaders, such as policy development, legal advice, communications, and issues management support. While a reasonable argument can be made that this support must be tailored to the policy and stakeholder realm of individual ministries, the same cannot be said of internal support services for public servants such as IT services, payroll, purchasing, and HR support. With the exception of human resources support, many "back office" services are transactional and generic, lending themselves to digitization, consolidation, and "shared service" models.

The most important investment in this area and a precondition for joint service delivery at all levels, is an enterprise-wide information technology system.

The most important investment in this area and a precondition for joint service delivery at all levels, is an enterprise-wide information technology system. This enables information-sharing across departments, which can support policy-making and communications consistency, and also supports front counter delivery to government clients. It is also much more cost-effective than running separate silo-based systems. This tends to be a fairly safe venue for consolidation and cost savings, given that it does not involve a reduction in visible front-line government services, and is a first choice for governments interested in building more integrated approaches to service delivery (Flaherty 2012; Morse 2013).

However, as demonstrated later in this book, the integration of public services tends not to be a linear process. For example, the Government of Canada has only recently embraced a shared back office model, despite being relatively advanced in integrating front counter services (Ambrose 2011).

Similarly, despite having a fairly comprehensive back office consolidation program and a growing online presence, the UK is much less advanced in co-locating offices and integrating front counter services.

SERVICE DELIVERY TO BUSINESS AND CITIZENS

Services to government clients have also been fragmented and duplicated, with up to three levels of government providing similar services without coordination, co-location, or even information sharing. Employment and labour market support has been a prime example in many countries. In many jurisdictions, including Canada, these services were duplicated by the federal, provincial, and municipal levels of government. In view of the high human impact, delivery costs and economic importance of this area, many jurisdictions, including the UK, Canada, Australia, US states, and Germany have prioritized this area for integration. In spite of some inter-jurisdictional consolidation of labour and employment services in Ontario, the province's 2012-13 budget revealed that eleven provincial ministries played some role in employment supports, and it committed to consolidating them. The same budget also noted that eight ministries were involved in providing support and grants to business. This function was also slated for consolidation (Duncan 2012).

The same is true of food inspections. In Canada, municipal public health units and provincial food inspectors enforce regulations where meat is being processed for in-province consumption. Federal food inspectors have jurisdiction over meat being processed for inter-provincial sale or export. Each level of government maintains its own specific regulations, inspectorate and back office support. This is mirrored in the regulation of waterways where interprovincial watersheds are federally regulated. In Ontario, shoreline regulation down to the water's edge is under provincial jurisdiction, while the waterway itself is federally regulated. Where a landowner improperly excavates a shoreline to build a dock or boat launch, both federal and provincial inspectors must be involved in on-site inspections and any necessary enforcement activity.

The issue of silos becomes even more important in the costly and complex world of human services. This is an area littered with examples of multiple needs clients of all ages engaging with a broad range of agencies and services, with little or no coordination or information sharing between those providing services. We still hear all too often about multiple needs clients requiring health and social service supports "falling through the cracks" between the dozen or so agencies with which they are in formal contact. We now know that is possible to describe and map these cracks because there are gaps both between organizations serving the same client base and in information held by the professionals working within them.

> **We still hear all too often about multiple needs clients requiring health and social service supports "falling through the cracks" between the dozen or so agencies with which they are in formal contact.**

FUNDING SILOS

Funding is also often siloed and subject to ministry or department level accountability rules. This is becoming a major pressure point in efforts to tackle pressing policy challenges. In aggregate, governments spend billions in an effort to tackle issues like poverty, mental health issues, Aboriginal education, domestic violence, and long-term unemployment. But in many cases, that funding is stovepiped through multiple policy and delivery organizations, usually at more than one level of government. Just as these tough social policy issues do not neatly align with the architecture of government, they are terribly ill-served by siloed funding. Furthermore, every one of those stovepipes has its own accountability and reporting requirements, together with an ever thickening web of rules associated with entitlement programs such as social assistance. Frances Lankin and Munir Sheikh's report on Ontario's social assistance regime explores this with a particular emphasis on employment supports. In addition to focusing a great deal on the fragmented nature of the ministries and agencies involved in these services, the reviewers note the importance of tackling the complex web of rules associated with social assistance. They "heard from caseworkers who could be spending 70 per cent of their time just administering the rules arising from the complex benefit structure – time they could be using, and want to use, to work directly with clients to help them achieve their employment goals" (Lankin and Sheikh 2012, 13).

On top of this, the risk-averse nature of political leaders who work in an intense 24/7 media spotlight inclines them to continually layer on new and "tougher" accountability requirements in the wake of every critical auditor's report or media exposé. Local public service leaders in both Canada and the UK identify overly-stringent accountability and reporting rules, together with inflexible funding structures that prevent movement across stovepiped allocations, as two of the most significant challenges they face in improving service delivery to citizens.

IMPLICATIONS FOR CITIZENS AND POLITICAL LEADERS

It is no surprise that citizens, business organizations, seniors' organizations, anti-poverty groups, and mental health advocates, to name just a few, find government to be complicated, confusing, and inaccessible. This is built right into its architecture. It is particularly the case where an issue or opportunity does not fall neatly inside the mandate of a single ministry, which is relatively common. Poverty reduction, mental health issues, and applications to commence mining exploration on Crown land that is subject to an aboriginal land claim are obvious examples. This complex distribution of accountability and interests often clouds responsibility when something goes wrong. There is no end of departments with an interest in a certain file or project but it's not always clear who is ultimately accountable.

Another layer of often-siloed services is found at the local level delivered by regional or municipal governments. This is especially so in the delivery of human services where a large number of agencies in the public, not-for-profit, and private sectors deliver an increasingly broad range of community and social services. These agencies take the accumulated weight of all the siloed activities above them in the constitutional hierarchy. They must also work with siloed policies, funding, and accountability requirements. Their funding often comes from a variety of sources – local, provincial, federal, and in some cases from charitable foundations. These funding streams are often allocated for discreet purposes or programs, and hence there is little flexibility to aggregate relatively small amounts of funding across budget lines to related activities. At the same time, these service delivery organizations, some of which are very small, must adhere to the often different accountability and audit requirements of each of their funders.

It is now broadly recognized both inside and outside government that it is government's responsibility make high quality public services accessible, affordable and sustainable.

In view of this fragmented and sclerotic architecture, it is easy to understand why gaps exist within and between ministries and agencies, and between the professionals who work in them. At the very end of this chain are citizens and service users who must, often with the help of family members, navigate their way through these siloed delivery systems. It is the spaces or gaps in between institutions or professional service providers through which vulnerable clients fall. Until recently, the onus has been on citizens to decipher government and publicly-funded services and to figure out how they can make those services work for them. It is now broadly recognized both inside and outside government that it is government's responsibility make high quality public services accessible, affordable and sustainable. This necessarily involves government adjusting to the needs of citizens and users.

A hopeful example of the challenges and nature of possible responses is described in a 2012 report published by the Local Government Association (2012, 6-7) in the UK. The report argues for a more integrated and personalized approach to delivering support for the estimated 260,000 young people who are most severely disengaged from work and training services. The report notes that there is no shortage of programs in this area. Young people between thirteen and twenty-four-years old can receive support from at least eight national organizations, funding thirty-three different funds and schemes, spanning thirteen different age groups – not including school funding – at a cost of over £15 billion each year. The report has proposed an integrated approach tailored to the individual client. This is encompassed by the following recommendations:

- A community budgeting approach to bring services together around the most disengaged. From the thirty-three funding streams we have indicated the six most suitable for pooling, creating a total budget of £1 billion a year.

- This would enable local partners to support the 260,000 most disengaged young people to be intensively supported back into work and learning, at a potential contribution of almost £4,000 each.

- A role for local partners in commissioning school, further education, and apprenticeship provision to enable the use of more innovative ways to tackle the issues and deliver much better results. (Local Government Association 2012, 7).

Siloed approaches to public service obviously do not result in the provision of optimal services to those in need of government services, nor do they provide value for the money taxpayers provide to government. In fact, it is probably the least effective and efficient way of designing a government or business enterprise. This has serious implications for service quality and affordability, and an impact on the ability of the elected government of the day to implement its political agenda. Furthermore, it thwarts efforts to build more engagement of citizens in policy-making and in electoral processes.

Government often moves slowly for political leaders, but issues or missteps can catch fire quickly and be hard to extinguish. One of the most common questions public service leaders will be asked by a political leader is, "Why does it take so long to get anything done around here?" It will hopefully be obvious by now that the answer lies in the architecture of government and its processes. The complexity and fragmentation in government also has important implications for the relationship between government and citizens.

The combination of multiple policy, program, delivery, funding, and accountability silos creates considerable distance and complexity between, for example, a prime minister or premier's priority initiative and front-line delivery staff and their clients. Together with distance, there are layers of opacity or thick curtains between government and the point of service delivery. As noted above, these agencies take the accumulated weight of all the siloed activities above them in the constitutional hierarchy. They must also work with siloed funding and siloed accountability requirements. Together these obstacles make it difficult for policy-makers to engage with citizens or front-line staff. It also leaves front-line staff and citizens wondering how government works, how decisions get made and how they can provide advice to the unfathomable government machine.

In 2009, I was appointed by Ontario's Minister of Labour to lead an expert panel inquiry into Ontario's workplace health and safety system. As the study unfolded, some familiar patterns emerged. Everyone was working hard within their organizational "silos of excellence" to protect worker safety, but the organizations in the system were not working together according to a common plan focused on clear priorities. They had no shared information system to enable risk identification, support policy-making, or help in tracking results. Further, there was no single point of accountability for the performance of the system. Our report and recommendations gave prominence to ways in which this siloed culture and organizational structure could be addressed, including the appointment of a Chief Prevention Officer as a single point of accountability for health and safety in the province (Expert Advisory Panel on Occupational Health and Safety 2010). This story is repeated over and over in the public sector. As noted above, reports on the SARS outbreaks in Toronto in 2003, in the aftermath of the 9/11 terrorist attacks, and on hurricane Katrina in 2005 tell similar stories.

Public service leaders and managers must constantly scan the landscape of policy actors both inside and outside the public service to ensure that dots are being connected. This is true at all levels of the organization, including the deputy minister level. As head of the public service in Ontario, I was surprised by the effort required to ensure coordination between the senior players of ministries that might have been expected to work together seamlessly. After an embarrassing Cabinet meeting at which one ministry had been nastily surprised by a related ministry's policy proposals I hauled the two responsible deputy ministers into my office with the message that none of us would leave the room until a shared protocol for proactive communications and collaboration between the two ministries had been worked out. This solved the problem and at the same time sent a message to other deputies that

The most significant opportunity for achieving gains lies in greater collaboration across organizational boundaries and in consolidating and integrating service at all levels.

they were expected to lead work and collaboration across boundaries as opposed to reinforcing silos. We will come back to the importance of leadership later in the book.

Siloed organizational structures and cultures are both inefficient and costly. They drain energy from the initial allocation of resources at every point. This is not fair for the public servants who work hard every day to collaborate in spite of silos, or for government service recipients who are not receiving the value they deserve. At the same time, there are emerging examples in several jurisdictions of new and exciting approaches to integrated services for multiple needs clients. The most significant opportunity for achieving gains lies in greater collaboration across organizational boundaries and in consolidating and integrating service at all levels. This includes standardizing high-volume repetitive tasks, while finding ways to tailor more complex human services to the specific needs of individuals. These initiatives are discussed in more detail in the following chapters.

THE ARCHITECTURE OF ACCOUNTABILITY

Before we leave the subject of architecture, it is important to briefly reference the hierarchical structure of accountability in government, particularly as it bears on political-administrative relationships. There is a well-established system of accountability in democratic governance which sees citizens delegating decision-making powers to elected representatives who in turn stand at the apex of a hierarchical "chain of command". Mark Jarvis explains that, "These superior-subordinate relationships cascade down the chain all the way from citizens as the ultimate superiors at the top, to 'street-level' bureaucrats who are responsible for implementing public policies and programs. In this way hierarchy establishes the democratic current that runs throughout contemporary systems of public governance and administration, linking the various actors, organizations and delegate responsibilities, while remaining accountable for the actions of their subordinates in the chain of command." (Jarvis 2014, 405-6).

The growth and dispersion of public sector operations, as well as the increasingly complex and collaborative nature of policy making and implementation is testing the limits of hierarchical accountability, making the work of political leaders, public service leaders and public servants more challenging. This is particularly so for a new generation of public servants as they make an effort to acclimatize to, and navigate within, already large, complex and mystifying organizations. This places an onus on public sector leaders to help as guides and interpreters of the landscape in which professional practice occurs. We revisit this in Chapter 8.

CHAPTER 4

THE SHIFT TOWARDS OPEN AND INTEGRATED POLICY AND DELIVERY

INTRODUCTION

This chapter examines an important shift towards more open and integrated policy-making and new approaches to implementing major political priorities. It begins with a brief discussion of policy-making and its intrinsic connection with the design and implementation of delivery mechanisms. This is again set in the context of the pressures bearing on the political and policy-making process. The meat of this chapter explores approaches to integration and networked policy-making within government and opening up the policy-making process to those outside government as part of a shift towards "co-production" (Bason 2010). The important role of evidence in policy-making is also discussed, including the potential for this to sometimes clash with political pressures and interests. In keeping with one of the key themes in this book I also draw attention to the skills that are important in a more networked and boundary-less world. Some conclusions are provided at the end of the chapter together with advice for practitioners.

POLICY-MAKING IN FLUX

Policy-making in the public sector supports government decision-making and, more recently, includes early thinking on the design and mechanics of implementing those decisions. The development of policy options and associated analysis assists government in moving forward with political priorities, addressing regulatory changes, delivering services to the public, and making other changes in public administration. Policy-making occurs at a number of levels – from broad economic policy developed by central agencies or finance ministries, to ministry-specific policies in all of the fields touched by government oversight and activity. Inter-governmental ministries develop policies regulating their government's policy and funding relationships with other levels of government, including the delegation of policy-making or delivery responsibility to a junior level of government or "uploading" those responsibilities to the senior level of government. Policy decisions are usually, although not always, reflected in legislation, regulations, and programs, which are sometimes referred to as policy instruments.

Policy options are supported by research, which can include document review, consultation, analysis and synthesis of information, and provision of options for decision-makers (Office of the Auditor General, Manitoba 2003). Options are normally evaluated against criteria that involve factors such as relative impact, cost, ease of implementation, anticipated stakeholders responses, and congruence with the political frame and commitments of the government.

The process of policy-making is influenced by many of the sweeping changes affecting the operation of governments and the work of public servants, including a constrained fiscal environment and citizen demands for better services. There has also been a growing acknowledgement by political leaders and senior public servants that complex challenges previously seen as intractable have become too burdensome and expensive to avoid. Obvious examples are poverty, homelessness, long-term unemployment, mental health, and multiple needs clients of health and social service agencies. These are all complex issues which cross ministry and, in many cases, jurisdictional boundaries.

In parallel – and especially for the realm of policy-making – citizens, partner organizations, and stakeholders are also calling for more accountability and transparency in government, a better understanding of how decisions are made, and for greater inclusion in the policy-making process. Bourgon has described this as a profound transformation in the relationship between citizens and the state, in which government is shifting from a role as insulated policy-maker to "one of co-creation and co-production of public goods with citizens" (2011, 33). There is now broad acceptance on the part of governments and public service leaders of the importance of working across government silos and engaging non-governmental actors and institutions in the process of policy-making and program design (Lindquist 2012; Pollitt 2012).

Collectively, these changes and pressures are transforming the policy-making environment, making the job of political leaders, policy analysts, and managers more complex and challenging. The government's hegemony over the policy-making process, and the data that informs it, is being seriously challenged. Policy-makers and policy communities are slowly adapting to these pressures. Policy renewal and improvement initiatives have become commonplace in public service organizations and are receiving attention from policy think tanks (Hallsworth and Rutter 2011). These discussions often culminate in checklists or best practices for practitioners. The Institute for Government, for example, describes some "policy fundamentals" considered integral to sound policy-making. They include: adequate definition of the issue or opportunity; the application of evidence and evaluation (with cost effectiveness, resiliency and risks); an appropriate accountability structure; and, a plan for rapid feedback and evaluation (2011, 14).

The shift to more joined-up and open government has been paralleled by the growth of research and writing on network management and the operation of networks in policy development and public service delivery. Scholarly writing on the application of network theory to public administration extends back to the early 1960s (Levine and White 1961). Network theory recognizes that public management and policy-making increasingly involves networks of actors and institutions working together across boundaries, as opposed to being hidden within the confines of a single hierarchical organization (Agranoff and McGuire 2003). In 1978, Scharpf concluded, "It is unlikely, if not impossible, that public policy of any significance could result from the choice process of any single unified actor. Policy formation and policy implementation are inevitably the result of interactions between a plurality of separate actors with separate interests, goals and strategies." (1978, 346). This description will be familiar to public service policy practitioners who are charged with consistently mapping networks of stakeholders and working to balance interests.

Network theory has explored the complex task of coordinating and managing networks of disparate actors engaged in policy-making and service delivery (Klijn 2005, 267-72). This includes the deployment of a number of different strategies, including interventions into pre-existing networks, motivating participants towards desired goals, and establishing coordinating mechanisms to maximize the value of interactions in achieving those goals (Agronoff and McGuire 2001; Koppenjan and Klijn 2004).

The Institute for Government's overview of policy-making touches on broader challenges and trends discussed throughout this book, including: more integrated approaches to policy-making inside government; experimentation with more open and collaborative policy-making with external stakeholders and service users; a greater emphasis on evidence and data in policy-making and in tracking progress towards priority goals; thinking about policy-making and implementation as part of a continuum, albeit one that is often nonlinear; and, the skill sets and experience required of the new generation of policy specialists, which crosses over to the importance of human resource management in general. This chapter explores each of these developments in turn.

INTEGRATED POLICY-MAKING IN GOVERNMENT

As discussed earlier, the ministry-based focus of Westminster models of government (and of fragmented agency structures in most countries) remains a major challenge to optimized policy and delivery. This is particularly the case in the high cost and high demand sphere of health and social service delivery. Alongside ministry-based silos it is common to find professional siloes in which policy-makers remain remote from professionals responsible for program delivery, and from legal and communications colleagues. Improving collaboration within government should be a priority area for public service leaders. It brings into play the importance of corporate approaches to priority files, challenges of accountability and the importance of building a collaborative culture. There is also a crossover to skills development.

Political and public service leaders have increasingly recognized that traditional approaches to problem solving and policy development have not been flexible and adaptive enough to tackle long term and seemingly intractable policy challenges in areas such as mental health issues, substance abuse, homelessness, long-term unemployment, and domestic violence. In view of the personal and social costs associated with these challenges, they have taken on new urgency for political leaders. As these issues assumed the status of political priorities two things became clear: first, none of them can be tackled by any one ministry or agency developing policy or designing delivery mechanisms alone; and secondly, addressing them comprehensively is beyond the capacity of government, even if it manages to operate as a fully integrated enterprise.

A comprehensive approach to tackling big policy challenges requires deep collaboration and joint working among several ministries as well as non-governmental organizations – some of which can be powerful domains in their own right. This is tough enough when there is a joint interest in addressing the needs of similar clients (for example, in social and children's services), but can be a greater challenge when there are perceived divergent interests between ministries (for example between ministries responsible for business growth and those responsible for environmental or labour regulation). In some cases, a minister responsible for a proposal to Cabinet might conceivably instruct his or her deputy minister to go it alone and thus avoid the messy complexity and delays of brokering compromises with a counterpart minister and ministry. These stories seldom end well.

These issues are broadly recognized but deeply entrenched. Several approaches have been developed to encourage more collaborative working. Some are entrepreneurial in the sense that two or more senior leaders collaborate because they know it is the right thing to do. While this should be encouraged and supported from the top of the organization, these efforts are usually situational and depend on the skills and personalities of incumbent leaders; this is not likely to evolve into systemic cultural change.

Beyond this, deputy ministers or assistant deputy ministers have routinely formed ad hoc inter-ministerial policy committees, and some of these take on a formal status. The Deputy Ministers' Social Policy Committee in Ontario is an established provincial example. The Canadian federal government has a broader and more formal Deputy Ministers' committee structure with mandates including public service renewal, economic trends and policies, and climate change, energy, and the environment. These are mandated to promote integrated policy development in priority areas; strengthen government-wide policy coherence; and, to pursue whole of government approaches to medium term management, human resources, and policy planning.[1] An inter-jurisdictional example is the Healthy People and Communities Steering Committee established by the Pan-Canadian Public Health Network. [2]

These committees are important fora for gathering and sharing information, and for discussing and developing policy on cross-ministry or cross-government initiatives. It is rare however, to see such committees advancing significant breakthrough policies or new modes of delivering public services. But they can certainly lend support and play a role in implementation where there is clear direction – and a clear mandate from the top of the organization, and preferably from both political and public service leaders.

A number of more tangible efforts have been made to incent cross-ministry collaboration. Mandate letters issued to newly-appointed ministers by political leaders are a promising development and have the potential to fill a number of gaps and clarify grey areas of accountability. In Canada, these letters have been used to describe the contribution that ministers and ministries are expected to make to both corporate and ministry-specific priorities (and sometimes to circumscribe inventiveness). Mandate letters also provide an opportunity to identify a lead policy minister where projects cross ministry boundaries, although this may require difficult internal political decisions and is thus sometimes avoided. These letters are not shared widely beyond the minister, usually seeing distribution to a small number of senior political staff and the appropriate deputy minister. An exception is the Canadian province of Alberta where, since 2012, mandate letters outlining the government's corporate priorities have been posted online.[3] In the province of Ontario, Premier Kathleen Wynne has since 2012 required cabinet ministers to countersign their mandate letters to signify formal acceptance of their mandate and mandate letters were made public in 2014.

I have watched governments of every political stripe struggle with cross-ministry accountability mechanisms at both the political and public service levels. In general, both levels talk a good game but are challenged with implementation. At the heart of this is an often unarticulated assumption that networked policy-making across organizational boundaries implies shared accountability for results. The success of these efforts are mostly situational and dependent on the leadership, brokering and navigational skills of the actors involved. A more consistent and predictable approach would require that explicit attention be given to accountability, incentives, and reporting on outcomes. I discuss this further in Chapter 8 on public service leadership where we touch on the importance of single points of accountability. An example from the UK is of interest here.

PUBLIC SERVICE AGREEMENTS IN THE UK

In 2007, at the tail end of the Blair government in the UK an initially small set of government-wide political priorities had ballooned to 120. These priorities were reflected in Public Service Agreements (PSAs). Each PSA was underpinned by a single Delivery Agreement, shared across all contributing departments and developed in consultation with delivery partners and front-line workers.[4] In 2007, Blair's successor, Gordon Brown, supported by the Prime Minister's Delivery Unit's (PMDU) new head, Ray Shostak, reduced the number of PSAs to thirty as part of an effort to bring clearer focus to the government's agenda. These included thorny cross-cutting issues such as poverty, the impact of drug and alcohol abuse, and income disparities. A group of national outcome-focused performance indicators was developed to measure the progress of each PSA.

Shostak put a great deal of thought into the accountability aspects of the revised PSAs, particularly on mechanisms that would encourage cross-ministry collaboration. Oversight of each PSA was assigned to a Cabinet subcommittee for discussion of cross-cutting issues, including those that could not be resolved by officials. Additionally, single points of political and public service accountability were assigned: political leadership was assigned to a minister of state who worked alongside a senior public servant responsible for delivery (a Senior Responsible Officer (SRO)). This arrangement was supplemented by cross-ministry boards and cross-ministry delivery agreements, both of which reinforced the importance of collaboration. In addition, separate incentives were put in place for SROs and permanent secretaries (the equivalent of deputy ministers in Canada). This was a sophisticated approach to design and incentives aimed at achieving collaboration across departmental lines with firm and identifiable lines of accountability.

OPEN GOVERNMENT, OPEN DATA AND CO-PRODUCTION IN POLICY-MAKING

Bourgon has noted the shift from government's role as hegemonic policy maker to "one of co-creation and co-production of public goods with citizens" (Bourgon 2011, 33). Political and public service leaders, policy think tanks, non-profit organizations, and social enterprises have reached the conclusion that governments do not have the capacity and resources to tackle big social issues in a monolithic way, especially not through command and control approaches to policy-making and delivery, and almost certainly not through traditional consultative mechanisms. The unprecedented wealth of information and the speed of its transfer through digitization has democratized policy-making. Digitization has huge implications for citizens, consumers, marketers, and political leaders.

The unprecedented wealth of information and the speed of its transfer through digitization has democratized policy-making.

Digitization has also been a driver in transforming public expectations about transparency, and access to information. There has been a steady move towards reporting on the quality and outcomes of public services. Easily accessible information on hospital wait times and student achievement are good examples. Ontario's Ministry of Transportation is using Bluetooth technology to help measure border wait times at critical crossings. Work is also under way to use crowd-sourced traffic flow data to provide real-time monitoring of traffic conditions. Data also drives improvement by shining a light on poorly performing institutions and by providing pointers about what makes others successful.

A related area of open government involves making both raw and processed data available for use by non-governmental organizations and individuals. DATA.GOV, the US government's open data portal, is a leading example of this. It outlines open government initiatives and provides links to almost 400 applications developed by citizens in contests and competitions to help others interpret raw government data. Similar open government initiatives are being launched by the government of Canada and the province of Ontario, which announced an open government program in 2013 and launched an online process for ideas on the provincial budget in 2015.

When information on service quality is made publicly available, it helps citizens make informed choices about government services. The UK government's July 2011 *White Paper on Open Government* set out its vision for reforming public services, focusing on increasing choices for service users, decentralizing power to the lowest appropriate level, opening up services to a range of providers, ensuring fair access to services and making public services accountable to users and taxpayers.[5] But the most significant, promising, and far-reaching element of open government lies in engaging citizens, government stakeholders, and service users in problem definition, research, policy-making, and program design. This is an area of huge demand from government stakeholders and service users (such as patient advocates), and is an equally large opportunity for government. Governments all over the world are realizing that they don't have all the answers to big policy problems, and are increasingly reaching out to local citizens, communities, and front-line delivery professionals for collaborative solutions, a process sometimes referred to as "co-creation" or "co-production" (Bason 2010). Alongside the benefits of harnessing the knowledge and skills of front-line service providers, delivery partners, and service users, this collaborative process of engagement has been linked to strengthening personal and community capacity and resiliency (Bourgon 2011, 84-88). A further advantage is that the process and outcomes of collaboration are depoliticized. It is hard to make a political football of community or expert-driven policies (although it is not impossible).

> The most significant, promising, and far-reaching element of open government lies in engaging citizens, government stakeholders, and service users in problem definition, research, policy-making, and program design.

Goldsmith and Eggers (2004) argued for a more porous and networked government in *Governing by Network*. Case studies supported their view that government leaders were already redefining their core responsibilities in a shift towards orchestrating networks of public, private, and non-profit organizations to design and deliver services previously tightly controlled by government. A shift in thinking in the latter years of UK Prime Minister Tony Blair's government resulted in a move away from central government control and towards user engagement and partnerships with front-line providers (Cabinet Office 2008). This was in part driven by fiscal pressures associated with the growing cost of health, community, family, and justice services, in parallel with rapidly shifting public expectations for better services. Political interest in this approach has been sustained by subsequent prime ministers Brown (Labour Party) and Cameron (Conservative Party).

CO-PRODUCTION IN REFORMING CONDOMINIUM LEGISLATION

A recent Canadian example of a more open approach to policy develop-ment is the review of Ontario's *Condominium Act* launched by the Ministry of Consumer Services in 2012. Ontario has seen a massive boom in condo-minium developments in the province, especially in Toronto, which in 2013 was the most active development site in North America. Condominiums account for almost half of new homes built in the province, and about 1.3 million Ontarians currently live in condos. Despite this, the governing statute for the sector remained unchanged for fifteen years. In that period, issues such as condominium design requirements, marketing rules, funding for maintenance, governance, training of building managers, and dispute resolu-tion approaches had not been comprehensively discussed or reviewed. These issues would bring to the foreground powerful and sometimes competing interests of developers, builders, managers, and owners. It also went to the heart of the ministry's mandate in finding a sensible balance between con-sumer protection and the promotion of responsible business practices.

In view of this complexity, and in large part due to the leadership of then deputy minister Giles Gherson, a decision was made to partner with the Ottawa-based Public Policy Forum to design an open and deliberative policy-making process, which involved the major non-governmental players from the outset. A three-stage collaborative public engagement process was developed and launched in 2012. The first phase, in the fall of 2012, involved hundreds of condominium sector stakeholders—owners, developers, property manag-ers, and others—meeting to talk about what changes they wanted to see in a modernized *Condominium Act*. The issues and solutions they identified were grouped into six categories: governance, dispute resolution, financial management, consumer protection, and condominium manager qualifications. The Public Policy Forum shared these and other findings in a public report in January 2013 (Public Policy Forum 2013).

The second stage began in March 2013, when experts reviewed the Stage One findings and began the process of developing options for renewing the Act. In the third stage in the fall of 2013, the options were reviewed and validated by condominium owners and other stakeholders, after which they were presented to the government and the condominium sector. Legislation has since been developed and was approved in June 2015. The process was highly successful, bringing together all major stakeholders at the front end to engage in identifying issues and talking through, contesting and brokering solutions. It worked well for the government: ministry officials say the exercise has brought expertise and capacity to the table that would have otherwise been beyond the reach of government. This was expertise it did not have internally and could not afford to buy.

It has also worked well for stakeholders and users. They were invited to the table at the outset and played a large role in shaping the agenda; they brought their issues and concerns forward together with their resources, knowledge, and expertise. They supported the initiative because they were legitimate partners in a process that was not being owned and controlled by government. Government was instead a convenor of conversations between sector owners and experts. In the language of Osborne, it is an example of public policy governance (2010, 6).

Municipal governments are moving in this direction, too. In July 2013, the City of Guelph, Ontario announced the creation of Canada's first municipal open government action plan. According to Mayor Karen Farbridge, the objective is to empower the community to "work together on innovative solutions and ultimately, all civic decisions … A tailor-made open government action plan developed for Guelph and co-produced with residents and businesses will position this plan to resonate locally and be used by other jurisdictions as a model for success" (Eggers and Macmillan, 2013, 175-201). The cities of Cologne, Germany, and Calgary, Alberta and the government of Ontario have also experimented with open "budget-building" programs.

In their 2013 book, *The Solution Revolution,* William Eggers and Paul Macmillan describe their view of the shift from silos and sectors to ecosystems, including discussion of where entrepreneurship and innovation ranges freely across sectoral boundaries. In this emerging system,

> The rigid silos of traditional industry, government – and even many foundations – run against the disruptive thinking of the solution economy. Rather than navigating fragmented hierarchies to advance an agenda, social entrepreneurs and organizational 'entrepreneurs' begin with the problem itself ... A core issue or objective, such as fighting malaria or revolutionizing higher education, becomes the centre of an ecosystem. As connected citizens share their concerns about, and interest in, the topic (in a conversation now made easier by the advent of social media and the Internet), market demand grows and enterprising contributors converge to meet the gap in the market (Eggers and Macmillan, 2013, 176).

The authors relate the ecosystem model to multi-sectoral approaches being developed to promote affordable housing and tackle human trafficking in developing regions of the world (Eggers and Macmillan 2013, 183-194).

A 2012 study by the UK-based Institute for Government (IFG) reviewed the country's National Planning Policy Framework and other models of more open policy-making (Rutter, 2012). It examined the experience of a Practitioners Advisory Group, which was established to draft a more streamlined planning process. Concerns with the Advisory Group experience led to IFG recommendations to government that included: transparency and clarity about the mandate of external groups and the process used in selecting participants; clarity about the status of work in progress and its relationship to the balance of the internal decision process going forward; involving other relevant government departments in the process; and addressing the concerns of groups and individuals left outside the process (Rutter 2012, 33).

The IFG noted, "All these new approaches require different skills from civil servants – who need to be prepared to be enablers and expert process designers rather than trying to monopolise the policy-making input behind closed doors. They also require ministers to be clear about areas that are off limits, but also to be prepared to engage with a much more open mind on issues that are in play. One of the clear conclusions from this report is that different ways of opening up have different benefits and problems. The idea that there is 'one model', which will work for the range of issues government deals with, is misguided. Better instead to have an appreciation of the range of options – and understand what works best for which issues and when" (Rutter 2012, 33).

THE IMPORTANCE OF DATA AND EVIDENCE

Data-driven policy has always been important in government. Previous generations of policy managers often lament the loss of research capacity and in-house government libraries. But the digitization of information and the speed of its transfer make huge amounts of information available to policy-makers. This is important because timely, solid, and relevant data drives sensible and useful policy options. As will be explored below, government doesn't always have the best data and is increasingly reliant on information from external researchers, think tanks, stakeholder organizations, universities, front-line professional managers and workers, and other levels of government. In the other direction, governments are realizing that opening their in-house information to external users informs better research and in many cases better local policy development and service delivery. There is an obvious connection between collaborative data sharing and collaborative policy-making. Data are also important in planning, monitoring and reporting on delivery, informing human resource management, and managing individual and work unit performance.

Good data is crucial to success in the policy development process, and its absence will normally have the reverse effect. Policy-making based on guesswork almost certainly results in under-achieving, over-achieving, or missing the target altogether. For example, on a holiday weekend in May 2000, E. coli contamination of drinking water serving the town of Walkerton, Ontario resulted in seven deaths and made 2,300 people ill, some chronically. Several layers of actors were involved, from local municipal water operators through to the provincial government, which has responsibility for regulating water safety. This was a major issue for the province at the time, as it occurred in the context of a move to smaller government and a very public emphasis on deregulation. The political reaction was swift and fairly typical. The government wanted to know what had happened, who was responsible, whether it could have been prevented, and how it could ensure that it didn't happen again. A high-profile public inquiry was launched, which subsequently found gaps in the regulatory and compliance system (O'Connor 2002).

In the aftermath of the Walkerton tragedy, the provincial government wanted to demonstrate that it was serious about tightening up the regulatory regime for drinking water in Ontario, and directed that relevant policy work be undertaken. Externally, a commitment was made that Ontario would have the safest drinking water in the world. Policy managers at the provincial Ministry of the Environment knew from the outset that this would be challenging. It was well known that large urban water facilities were well managed, tightly regulated, and subject to a rigorous inspection regime. Risk increased at smaller water facilities, in remote rural areas (which were often under "boil water" advisories), and in small communities, homes, and businesses (such as gas stations) drawing water from private wells. Given the hugely dispersed population of Ontario, an obvious step in parsing out and prioritizing levels of risk across the province would be to draw on hydrogeological data in order to map areas at risk of groundwater contamination.

But at that stage the public service advised that the data were not comprehensive enough to inform a risk-based approach to regulation. With public, media, and political pressures rising, the government of the day felt that it had little choice but to move ahead in developing one-size-fits-all regulations and to base these on conservative assumptions that veered on the side of public safety. While representatives from small, targeted communities warned about unforeseen and costly impacts on low-risk consumers, the predominant view inside government was that it was better to be seen to over-achieve than under-achieve. Over the following few months as the specific causes of the contamination became clear, more data were generated and a significant outcry was being heard from small water well users and local utility operators based on the increased costs of new construction and maintenance standards, inspections, and reporting. This prompted reconsideration and, eventually, scaling back of the original suite of water regulations. This was the worst-case scenario for a government that had committed to toughen-up the regulations.

Evidence-based policy has been practiced for a long time, for example in public health. In 1854, Dr. John Snow used a dot-map to identify clusters of cholera cases in London, England, finding that a water pump in Soho was the source of the contamination. Cholera had previously been associated with pollution or "bad air" and Snow's finding has been called a founding event in the science of epidemiology. In the 1990s, New York City's Police Commissioner Bill Bratton introduced computer-based statistics to track crime incidents and spot emerging patterns early. Comprehensive strategies were developed to deal with significant crime trends and local unit commanders were held to account for results. This practice is now commonplace in policing.

Eggers and Macmillan recount the following story from Chicago: "In October 2010, Chicago Police Department's new Predictive Analysis Group was analyzing emergency calls. It printed a report showing that a shooting was likely to occur on a particular block on the South Side. Just minutes later, Brett Goldstein, director of the group, felt his Blackberry vibrate. The text reported a murder ... He checked the time stamps. The data had predicted the murder three minutes before it had happened" (Eggers and Macmillan 2013, 65-66).

The use of data to identify potential problems and to predict outcomes is reflective of a more proactive or anticipatory role for government. Investing in anticipative capacity positions governments to detect emerging trends and design proactive preventative interventions, or to divert emerging forces towards more desirable outcomes.

Over the past couple of decades there has been a renewed emphasis inside and outside government on the substantial role of evidence in policy development. This has been driven by a number of factors, including the large increase in the number of organizations trying to influence government with evidence, such as professional bodies, think tanks and university researchers. There has also been a proliferation of social scientific knowledge, which is more aligned with policy priorities. On the surface, governments have responded positively. Ontario's Ministry of Health is building on the practice of evidence-based medicine in its promotion of evidence-based approaches to health care. Evidence also figured significantly in the UK's "Modernizing Government" initiative which, as discussed, has been supported by three consecutive prime ministers. Canada's federal government has also endorsed the importance of evidence in policy-making, although as of 2015 it was being broadly criticized for downplaying evidence and science in policy-making (the field of justice policy and the elimination of the long-form census are among the more graphic examples).

Governments' enthusiasm for more rigor and evidence in policy-making reflects the rapidly changing and more complex character of the issues facing political leaders and the pressure they are feeling to deliver results. UK Prime Minister Tony Blair insisted on better evidence to drive student performance and the reduction of waiting times for important diagnostic tests and surgeries. It worked in the sense of measuring progress along a time-based trajectory and in holding delivery officials to account for results (Barber 2007). Two further additional data-driven approaches to policy-making are worth detailed examination.

"TROUBLED FAMILIES" IN THE UNITED KINGDOM

In the wake of extensive riots involving young people across the UK in 2011, Prime Minister David Cameron, asked for data on the nation's "troubled families", which, in subsequent research, were defined as high-volume users of justice, social and children's, and mental health services. By examining multiple sources of data government researchers identified 120,000 family units which have since been targeted for enhanced government support and interventions. It is estimated that £9 billion is spent annually on these families, or an average of £75,000 per family. Of that total, £8 billion is spent on reactive strategies and amelioration, with only £1 billion being spent on helping families to solve and prevent problems in the longer term.[6] For the first time, the government moved beyond anecdotal descriptions of troubled families. It now has a sense of the make-up of the families and where they live. Not surprisingly, many are clustered in high-crime neighbourhoods in low-income areas of cities throughout the UK, and many troubled families are related to each other. The study also highlighted the importance of mapping total spending on significant social issues and the nature of that spending.

As an outcome of this research, a Troubled Families program was launched by the prime minister in 2011. Louise Casey, who was appointed to lead the program, published a report in 2012 highlighting the chaotic personal histories of some troubled families.[7] A further report on the benefits of intensive intervention was completed by the National Centre for Social Research[8] and in 2012 a "Troubled Families" team published a report on the academic evidence associated with family intervention strategies.[9] The Troubled Families team, based in the Department for Communities and Local Government (DCLG) was established to integrate efforts across the whole of government and to provide expert help to local authorities in implementing the program. According to the department's web site, the program will work with local government to reintegrate children back into school, tackle youth crime, and support adults in finding employment. The goal of reducing the overall costs of providing currently fragmented services to these families is being paralleled with an effort to better equip local service providers to work with families in a more holistic way, including appointing a single caseworker to each family to provide intensive and ongoing support. Financial incentives include an increase in local authority budgets by £448 million over three years with payments being based on measurable outcomes.

This is a useful example of a central government using multiple sources of data to map the characteristics of a complex and expensive inter-generational social challenge. From a delivery perspective there is a clear leaning towards local and community-based responses incented and supported by central government funding.

REDUCING HEALTH WAIT TIMES IN ONTARIO

Shortly after his election in 2013, Ontario Premier Dalton McGuinty adopted reduced wait times for key medical diagnostics and surgeries as one of a small number of political priorities on which he and his government were prepared to be judged. I was present at an early meeting of a high-powered health results team when McGuinty asked for current wait-times data on the targeted procedures. There was a nervous pause before the premier was told by an embarrassed public service manager that standardized data on wait times were not readily available. McGuinty was told that while many hospitals tracked wait times for some procedures, this was not done consistently across the province. Standardized benchmarks were not available as a starting point from which to measure progress. Getting those benchmarks in place took several months – a large bite out of a four-year political mandate. Nevertheless, the investment was sound and there was confidence that the change process was being launched with purpose-built data and an efficient process for tracking and reporting on it. Unlike the more complex and crisis-ridden Walkerton example, there was time to invest in generating decent data. There would be no gaps and no guesswork.

> ... requirements for throughput, quality, and costs could be standardized across the system with funding increases being used as an incentive to encourage low-performers to adopt demonstrably successful practices.

The baseline data on wait times were useful in tracking progress towards McGuinty's political priority but their fuller potential became evident relatively quickly. The data raised questions about why some hospitals were more efficient in patient throughput than others, and about why there were substantial variances in both the quality and unit cost of procedures. Quality and costs mattered a lot because the targeted procedures included both diagnostics and surgeries for cancer and coronary conditions. While it might be assumed that longer wait times could be associated with higher quality procedures, this was not necessarily the case. Some hospitals with short wait times also demonstrated higher quality outcomes and low unit costs. The big question was, "why?"

This question prompted a close examination of what made successful hospitals successful. Once these factors (i.e., a mix of planning, work processes, procurement, and inter-professional collaboration) were identified, these practices could be shared with lower-performing hospitals. Furthermore, requirements for throughput, quality, and costs could be standardized across the system with funding increases being used as an incentive to encourage low-performers to adopt demonstrably successful practices. To be fair to the low performers, they had no idea how their performance ranked in relation to other hospitals before someone started counting. This is a powerful example of the importance of data and evidence.

Don Drummond highlights this further in his 2012 report on reforming Ontario's public services, making the connection between evidence-based policy, data-driven monitoring and reporting, and the assessment of individuals and departments in meeting objectives (2012, 127). Drummond discussed further opportunities for public service transformation in the large and expensive service delivery sectors. In the health system, he pointed to the importance of research-based clinical practice guidelines to support physicians in keeping pace with research and best practices. He suggested that these guidelines could also help in guiding decision-making on procedures that should be listed or not for public insurance coverage. Drummond emphasized the need for collaboration with physicians, research organizations, and other levels of government as part of an effort to ensure that directives are not unreasonably rigid (2012, 185-6). He explored additional examples of evidence-driven approaches to transformation in other important areas of delivery such as special education (2012, 225) and labour market development (2012, 283).

EVIDENCE-BASED POLICY MEETS POLITICAL REALITY

While the importance of evidence in policy-making and in delivery has been elevated in recent years, some controversy has also emerged on the degree to which political leaders have been open to reliance on evidence in decision-making. Policy-making is not always linear or even rational (although it can be when all of the necessary political and public policy tumblers line up to make it a winning proposition). Practitioners know that the policy process can also be contested and messy, with powerful stakeholders marshalling robust data to argue for different outcomes. Sometimes policy decisions are based on flimsy evidence or are formulated to meet short-term political interests such as pandering to a core of supporters – a criticism often made about governments that pursue "tough-on-crime" agendas in the face of declining crime statistics. While seasoned public servants will understand this sort of ambiguity, the scientific community, as well as some newer and more idealistic public servants, find it tougher to swallow. In addition, some of the breakthroughs anticipated from rigorously data-driven policy-making have not materialized. There is useful research and writing on the issues and challenges associated with evidence-based policy-making.

Nutley et al. (2010) and Head (2010) have conducted cross-jurisdictional research in exploring debates on the potential role of different types of information, how evidence is used to inform policies and practices, and questions of "ownership" of both the evidence agenda and the evidence base. Nutley and Head share the observation that policy-making, with its multiple lenses and interests, is always more chaotic and political than "evidence" implies. Head pragmatically concludes that "evidence-informed" policy might be a better alternative than the hope that evidence will mechanically drive policy decision-making. He offers five reasons for this. First, in many cases there is insufficient data available to policy makers and political leaders, especially when initial research reveals layers of complexity and further gaps in knowledge. Nutley adds that there is less status and fewer incentives for academics engaging in policy and practice-relevant work than in publishing in traditional peer-reviewed journals (2010, 142).

Second, it is natural that policy managers and political leaders are influenced by a multitude of factors alongside research and evidence. Head notes that "the availability of reliable research does not ensure its subsequent influence and impact" (2010, 80). Political leaders are often preoccupied with maintaining support among allies, responding to media commentary, and managing risks.

Third, it is not unusual to see translation challenges or "poor fit" between how data has been compiled and presented and the real-time needs of policy managers. Head notes, "Researchers themselves are not adept at packaging and communicating their findings, and may prefer to remain distant from direct engagement with public debates around key issues" (2010, 80).

Fourth, the policy process is starting to open up to a broader range of participants and the value of professional knowledge, as opposed to research-based knowledge, is increasingly seen as an important input. Professionals deal with complex problems on the ground and are seen as well-positioned to learn by adjusting central prescriptions to local conditions. As a result, policy managers must deal with a broader range of information inputs and must weigh their relative importance (2010, 80).

Fifth, Head observes that the role of evidence will often be much more fragile and malleable on policy files that are turbulent, or subject to rapid changes. "Here, evidence-based arguments are likely to become politicized and evidence will be used for partisan purposes" (2010, 81).

Head points to four key enabling factors that could better underpin a more robust and systematic approach to evidence-informed policy:

1. The development of high quality information;
2. Developing policy professionals with skills in data analysis and policy evaluation (speaking again to the importance of HR development);
3. The establishment of organizational and political incentives to promote the adoption of evidence-informed approaches; and,
4. The development of stronger relationships between producers and users of research (2010, 81-82).

On the last point, there is widespread agreement that the research and policy-making communities have lots of room to work with each other more effectively. Research should be more attuned to major policy challenges and opportunities and effectively translated, shared with, and communicated to policy makers. At the other end, policy makers must be proactive in building relationships with key researchers and institutions and in signalling research needs to those communities. They must also become more adept in locating, interpreting, and applying research to inform policy and practice.

Head describes weaving strands of information and values through the lens of scientific research, professional experience, and political judgement with the result that, "There is not one evidence-base but several bases. These disparate bodies of knowledge become multiple sets of evidence that inform and influence policy rather than determine it" (2008, 1).

THE POLICY-IMPLEMENTATION CONTINUUM

Historically, many governments have believed (rightly or wrongly) they make good policies, but readily acknowledge they have been challenged in implementation (Pressman and Wildavsky 1973). Implicit in this, at least until recently, has been some comfort for governments that they are getting the important part right but that those responsible for on-the-ground delivery are screwing things up. In many cases, implementation has worked because policy makers have engaged delivery professionals at the design stage or have had front-line experience themselves. It is also the case that some policies are just easier to implement than others. Challenges arise in efforts to promote behaviour change (for example, in injury prevention), or in the relatively complex areas of health and human services and justice services. As noted earlier, effective implementation is also challenged by the length and complexity of the chain of organizations and actors involved in delivery.

Policy implementation has seen breakthroughs over the past fifteen years, as a result of an outcomes-based emphasis on new managerial practices, citizen demands for better services, and the growing impatience of political leaders who are increasingly held to account for measurable results.[10] The move to a focus on outcomes has forced changes to planning, policy development and how budgets are developed and implemented. The UK has been a pacesetter in this area starting with the creation of the PMDU in 2001 (Barber, 2007) and with the later development of priority-based Public Service Agreements.

One of the preconditions for successful delivery is establishing a small number of priorities and driving these relentlessly. Establishing priorities publicly can create pressure for both collaboration and focused implementation, especially where targets are made public. Michael Barber, who created Blair's delivery unit, describes his early conversations on prioritization with Blair in *Instruction to Deliver* (2007). The genesis of this approach to delivery lay in Blair's early commitments to dramatically improve literacy at the primary level. As the story goes, Blair greatly enjoyed the first several months of his first term in office pulling the levers of change in government – only to find that the levers were not connected to anything. The mix of Blair's commitment to public service reform, impatience for results, and willingness to personally monitor delivery underpins the story that followed.

In 2001, Blair identified several key priorities in four departments: key health wait times; literacy, numeracy and truancy; crime; and, transport (rail punctuality and road congestion), with responsibility for monitoring and driving delivery going to the PMDU, housed in the Cabinet Office and reporting directly to the prime minister. Barber describes key success factors as:

- a close identification of the delivery unit with the prime minister;

- emphasis on establishing clear goals and associated "delivery maps";

- analyses of delivery chains and data driven trajectories;

- periodic "stocktaking" meetings led by the prime minister involving uncompromising progress reports; and,

- a close relationship with the Treasury department to align spending with desired outcomes.

This approach acknowledged that complex problems require a multiplicity of approaches in combination, with trial and error informed by rapid data feedback. It equally recognized that significant change requires long and grinding work (Barber 2007; Collins 2001 and 2005).

In its early days, the PMDU was considered to be tackling areas of organizational inertia as well as an absence of rigorous problem-solving and project management skills at the departmental level. Consequently, Barber's team operated in a command and control style, driving hard from the centre of government. While unpopular with front-line professionals and some government departments, the new approach to delivery was highly successful in getting results in priority areas, at least in the short term. There were rapid improvements in literacy as well as a significant narrowing of the gap between advantaged and disadvantaged students. Key health wait times were reduced, and there was a marked increase in train reliability and punctuality. A more general breakthrough was a shift to a culture based on prioritization and outcomes. This was achieved through tough decisions on priority setting, a relentless drive to examine and influence complex delivery chains, and frequent, energetic stocktaking by prime ministers. Prompted in part by the disengagement of departments and front-line delivery professionals, UK delivery leaders, especially Barber's successor Ray Shostak, looked at emerging delivery practices in other countries,

Key health wait times were reduced, and there was a marked increase in train reliability and punctuality.

including some Australian states and Ontario's experience. These jurisdictions had based their reformed delivery techniques partly on the PMDU model but chose to experiment with more inclusive approaches. A significant change in direction followed in the UK. Capacity for delivery was strengthened at the departmental level alongside an effort to work more closely with professional service providers, especially in the health and education sectors. A new emphasis was also placed on engaging the views of citizens in the roles as users of public services. This transition also saw a shift to measuring quality as much as quantity. This transition is reflected in a 2008 Cabinet Office report for then Prime Minister Gordon Brown called "Excellence and Fairness: Achieving World Class Public Services" (Cabinet Office 2008).

Michael Barber had recognized this necessary evolution in 2004: "To pick up the argument I made to Cabinet in December, 2004, command-and-control done well can rapidly shift a service from 'awful' to 'adequate'. This is a major achievement, but not good enough because the public are not satisfied with 'adequate' – they want 'good' or 'great'. But command-and-control cannot deliver 'good' or 'great' for, as Joel Klein, Chancellor of the New York City Department of Education, puts it , 'You cannot mandate 'greatness'; it has to be unleashed'" (2007, 334-5).

In Canada, Ontario's Premier Dalton McGuinty made his health and education priorities explicit early in his first mandate starting in 2003, together with highly-specific and measurable goals. Together with considerable personal leadership effort from McGuinty and the support of a high-profile delivery team, these initiatives were successful in generating intra-sectoral collaboration and successful outcomes. From 2004-2008, Ontario made systematic delivery breakthroughs in the education and health areas with premier-led "Results Teams" using measurement and stocktaking methods based on UK practices. An Ontario "delivery unit" was created but ministries maintained the lion's share of accountability for execution. Delivery units focusing on climate change have also been established in the Cabinet Offices of British Columbia and Ontario. These approaches appear to have worked well but there are questions about the extent to which emerging knowledge and innovation is being systematically captured.

SKILLS FOR POLICY-MAKING

High-level strategic approaches to human resource development are important enablers of high performance organizations. Top-flight policy-making in the turbulent and unpredictable world of government requires that policy professionals have the right training, skills, and resources. Within government, policy-making is considered to be at the peak of the professional skills hierarchy, but until recently with the new breed of well-trained graduate students emerging from policy schools, most policy professionals have grown their skills on-the-job. In view of the challenges facing governments and citizens, public service leaders must turn their minds to the skills required for successful policy-making and ensuring that these are reinforced and communicated to policy professionals (Dean 2009).

In particular there should be a sustained focus on building capacity for tackling complex and cross-cutting policy challenges with a focus on "boundary-spanning skills".

In particular there should be a sustained focus on building capacity for tackling complex and cross-cutting policy challenges with a focus on "boundary-spanning skills" (Lodge and Malinowski 2007). The skills of emerging "networked public policy professionals" should include the ability to comfortably network and collaborate with stakeholders, service users, front-line professionals, academics, and consultants. They should be adept at negotiation and problem solving, building and managing transitory project teams, collaborating across professional and organizational boundaries, and seamlessly integrating policy, strategy, implementation planning, and delivery. In view of the importance of data and evidence in policy-making and service delivery, there must also be an understanding of the importance of signalling the need for priority-based research and data outwards to the academic and broader research community, and to ensuring that resulting research is effectively translated before reaching government. Given the growing number of sources of data and advice, policy practitioners must be adept at sorting through multiple sources of data, validating them, and quickly translating them into advice for decision-makers.

One of the largest learning gaps in most jurisdictions continues to be in the effective transfer of knowledge between senior and junior staff and between front-line delivery professionals and policy departments. This requires effective knowledge management strategies, benefiting from knowledge already existing in the organization as well as the ability of public sector organizations to capture and share innovative practices. In some cases this can be supported by the creation of central organizations specifically mandated for this purpose (Lodge and Malinowski 2007), or building on current informal communities of practice in public service organizations already providing learning opportunities.

As a starting point, public service leaders who are responsible for the capacity of their organizations should be clear about the qualities required for successful policy-making, and should determine, to the extent possible, the degree to which these are present. Identifying and filling significant gaps should be a priority. This speaks once again to the importance of human resource strategy and management.

CONCLUSIONS

Policy-making is a core business of government but the practice of policy-making is changing in response to changes in the economy, the expectations of citizens, stakeholders, and service users, and an expanding marketplace of policy inputs. This is an important moment for democratic governments as they experience reduced control over the policy-making and communications environment. The process of co-production in policy-making moves beyond traditional notions of joined-up government. It implies instead the possibility of a more boundary-less vision of policy development, which involves users of services, delivery professionals, academics, non-profit, private sector experts, and front-line public servants in shaping the issues, gathering, sharing, and contesting data, and then brokering workable and realistic policy options.

There is still too much siloed policy-making in government and this will always result in sub-optimal approaches to problems or opportunities that cross organizational boundaries. Building a culture in which public servants work seamlessly across borders is a political and public service leadership imperative at every level of government. In this context, Evert Lindquist puts it plainly in noting that a horizontal mindset is a prerequisite for those working in the public sector (2002, 153). This is one of the key requirements for collaborative, just-in-time, policy development that is responsive to the growing expectations of stakeholders, experts, partners, and service users – and for bringing their knowledge, expertise, and various other forms of capital to policy-making tables.

Without good data, policy-making is little more than guesswork and the outcomes will usually reflect that.

Associated with this more open approach to governance is the rapidly growing practice of making government data more available to external researchers for their use and re-use. Digitization has made real-time data sharing possible as well as providing for sophisticated analytics.

The availability of solid and relevant data will often drive sensible policy options, and can empower governments to unpack previously unfathomable problems. Without good data, policy-making is little more than guesswork and the outcomes will usually reflect that.

Beyond supporting policy-making, data is essential in supporting implementation – for measuring progress towards desired outcomes and informing the need for necessary adjustments. In other words, it provides for a much more iterative approach to delivery as opposed to the traditional assumption that if we get the policy right everything else will be fine.

Evidence based policy-making has been elevated in recent years, if not heralded as the perfect meeting place of democracy and technocracy. In practice, most policy makers understand that the decision-making processes of government are not as linear, rational, and evidence-based as many would hope. Brian Head and Sandra Nutley have explored the supply and demand aspects of evidence, its contestability, and the often turbulent and complex context in which policy decisions are made and implemented. The advice that evidence-informed policy is probably a more realistic expectation is practical and sensible.

There has been a longstanding gap between policy and implementation. Pressure for more effective and measurable delivery has caused political leaders to demand better results. The UK's systematic efforts to achieve effective delivery on political priorities in change-resistant sectors such as health and education have been groundbreaking. It is now widely acknowledged that command and control approaches to delivery might be useful in responding to crises but are not sustainable in building long-term improvements in service delivery. A more balanced, collaborative, and capacity-building approach has now evolved which incorporates mapping of collaborative possibilities across sectors and jurisdictions, and greater involvement of providers and end users, all in combination with some form of rallying cry towards a virtuous moral purpose – such as improving educational outcomes for children. This approach has been successfully tested in Ontario.

ADVICE FOR GOVERNMENTS, LEADERS AND PRACTITIONERS

- Governments in Canada have recognized the imperatives of greater collaboration across ministry, professional, and jurisdictional boundaries, and of a more open approach to policy-making and program design. Progress is slow and must be accelerated. Leaders at every level of the organization should establish expectations for integrated cross-boundary policy work. Examples of success (and failure) should be highlighted as learning opportunities. Examples from our own organizations demonstrate that cross-boundary policy-making is already happening in our context, what it looks like and the factors that made it successful, including how risks were managed. This will also connect successful practitioners in various ministries and start the process of building a specific community of practice.

- Governments are dealing with both shrinking resources and citizen demands for better services. Opening up policy-making and program design to external stakeholders, delivery professionals, and service users provides government with a sizeable source of professional and community expertise, as well as maintaining or improving the resiliency of citizens and communities.

- Many policy makers are attuned to the importance of successful delivery – especially in relation to significant political priorities. Getting policies and new initiatives off the page and into action continues to be a challenge in many organizations. Canadian and other jurisdictions now have considerable experience in driving the delivery of political priorities. Critical factors in successful delivery are: top level political support; establishing and sustaining a clear focus; applying clear and simple methods; getting the right people in the right positions, securing good collaboration between departments, building and maintaining routines which drive performance; and transparency – including the effective use of data to measure progress and inform the need for course corrections.

- Establishing a short list of a premier's or prime minister's top level political priorities is a prerequisite for effective delivery, as is their involvement in monitoring progress. Command and control delivery systems have a place as part of a suite of delivery approaches, but they are not a panacea. Recent experiences with more collaborative models in Ontario and the shift to a more collaborative approach to delivery in the UK provide some guidance for practitioners.

- Current and relevant data and research are critical for assessing risk in regulatory regimes, informing policy development, benchmarking and tracking efforts to implement political priorities, and improving service delivery. Data are also being used to help unpack previously intractable issues such as in the UK "troubled families". Public service leaders must ensure that there is sufficient capacity within their organizations (or that it is readily available externally) to maximize these opportunities. Additionally, policy makers must be more proactive in signalling priority areas for research to producers of knowledge, as well as providing guidance and support on how knowledge can be translated for use by policy-makers, political staff, and political leaders.

- Building capacity for stronger policy-making and implementation necessarily involves skills development. Public service leaders must ensure that human resource strategies place emphasis on developing skills for open and boundary-less policy-making. Policy practitioners must be comfortable networking and collaborating with stakeholders, service users, front-line professionals, academics, and consultants. They are normally cast in the role of integrators of the advice of several other professions (legal, finance, communications, etc.), and must also be competent in quickly accessing data from multiple sources and translating this into options and advice for decision-makers.

CHAPTER 5

THE CROSSOVER BETWEEN DEFICIT REDUCTION PROGRAMS AND PUBLIC SERVICE REFORM

This chapter turns to government responses to fiscal deficits, with an emphasis on Canada and a particular focus on the intersection of deficit reduction strategies with public service reform. It distinguishes between across-the-board approaches to budget cuts and staff reduction targets, and policy-based or "transformational" approaches which seek to prioritize, sustain, and improve the public services that matter most to citizens. The former approach is arguably influenced by new public management and neo-liberal views on the role of the state (Shields and Evans 1998), while the latter postulates a more innovative, activist, and networked public sector (Pollitt and Bouckaert 2011), as well as a public sector in which efficiency and effectiveness is maximized (Hjartarson et al. 2014). I have seen both of these approaches deployed in government and will reflect on that experience below.

The starting point for policy-based approaches to public service reform is that there is plenty of scope to improve public services with or without fiscal pressures. As Canadian economist Don Drummond has pointed out, improving public services and providing better value for money should always be a priority, even in the absence of big deficits (2012). Indeed, in view of the size of the public sector in Canada it is an obvious place to look for efficiencies and especially those that maintain or improve important public services.

It is helpful to begin by looking at the pressures that have given rise to the focus on deficits and the range of approaches available to governments in tackling them. The Canadian experience with productivity and deficit reduction programs is then reviewed with a particular emphasis on the federal government's widely applauded Program Review exercise in the mid 1990s. The chapter then reviews three recent reports dealing with approaches to deficit reduction, which provide some guidance for public sector leaders and practitioners.

PRESSURES FOR REFORM

We have explored pressures driving public service reform in Chapter 1. While previously cyclical in nature, fiscal deficits have become a semi-permanent feature of the North American and European landscape following the banking crisis of 2007-2008. In Canada, these pressures have been compounded by the acceleration of global competition and the resulting decimation of the country's manufacturing base. As I write this early in 2015, crude oil prices have fallen by 50 per cent and the province of Alberta is reeling from a steep drop-off in resource revenues. A multi-billion dollar budget surplus is fast descending into deficit territory.

On top of this, demographically driven demands for more, better, and increasingly expensive services in the high-spending areas of health, social, and community services are driving costs up at the same time as revenue growth is slowing. Governments are being forced to address both cyclical and structural deficits, and this in turn will require significant changes to the structure and operations of government (Mendelsohn et al. 2010). Some of these changes are already under way (Pollitt and Bouckaert 2011), but will need to be deepened and accelerated. While Canada has fared better than many OECD countries it cannot be complacent and this is particularly the case at the provincial level (TD Economics 2014). Quebec and Ontario, its two largest provinces, have larger debts and debt-to-GDP ratios than most other provinces and a good many countries. Ontario in particular faces an uphill battle to return to fiscal balance (Drummond 2012).

Unlike previous recessions in the 1970s and 1980s, the current underlying fiscal gaps are not sustainable. Nor can it be assumed that budget deficits will be corrected when the recession ends and growth returns to historical levels. Difficult decisions will be required to reduce spending and to find palatable means of raising more revenues.

APPROACHES TO DEFICIT REDUCTION

Governments have taken three approaches to addressing deficits or achieving fiscal sustainability: raising revenues through taxes or user fees; across-the-board spending cuts or by specific program cuts; and rethinking the role and shape of government and how services are delivered. This third approach is sometimes referred to as a "transformative" approach to sustainability (Mendelsohn et al. 2010). Drummond notes that arbitrary spending and job cuts seldom have a lasting impact. He is blunt in saying, "The only way to get out of deficits and stay out, in a period of limited economic growth, is to reform government programs and the manner in which they are delivered" (2012, viii). Under this approach, no assumptions are made about the right size of government, so it avoids establishing up-front projections of job and program cuts. Rather, it assumes that government as a whole is not working as well as it should be, in part due to siloed approaches to policy-making, program design, funding, and the delivery of public services (Dean and Boutilier 2012).

Drummond emphasizes, "Much of this task can be accomplished through reforms to the delivery of public services that not only contribute to deficit elimination but are also desirable in their own right. Affordability and excellence are not incompatible; they can be reconciled by greater efficiency, which serves both the fiscal imperative and Ontarians' desire for better-run programs" (2012, 1).

PROGRAM REVIEW IN CANADA

In various forms, governments in western democracies have been forced to take a more active role in public policy and management as a result of economic challenges, the loss of public confidence in government, and a simultaneous increase in public expectations for more efficient and effective public services (Aucoin 1995, 2). Partly in reaction to this, the management of finances together with policy and communication have been increasingly centralized (Savoie 1999). Parallel efforts have been made to decentralize authority over allocated budgets in order to achieve local efficiencies (Aucoin 1995, 9). In the Canadian context, a number of efforts have been made to control government finances and, over time, to actively review government programs for efficiency and effectiveness.

In 1930, an office of the Comptroller of the Treasury was established as part of the government of Canada's finance portfolio, charged with the task of putting in place a centralized system of financial management. Further entrenched over the following decades, it was eventually called into question in the mid-1960s Glasco Commission on Government Organization, which recommended decentralization of some management authority – in the style of the new public management that was to follow a couple of decades later (Aucoin 1995, 101).

The first dedicated effort at a program review function in Canada emerged under the Mulroney conservative government's Ministerial Task Force on Program Review. In the context of fiscal challenges, about one thousand programs were reviewed, with recommendations finding their way into the 1985 budget. But without the necessary political will to implement the recommendations the government reverted to across-the-board spending cuts. A similar effort in 1988 saw the creation of an Expenditure Review Committee, reporting to the powerful Operations Committee of Mulroney's cabinet. This effort failed as a result of a backlash from ministers, and was dissolved four years later (Aucoin 1995, 117-8).

A great deal of experience in program review has been developed at the provincial level but perhaps the most widely known model was implemented by the Chrétien Liberal government in the mid-1990s in the context of an earlier fiscal crisis, which saw the government of Canada's debt reach 67 per cent of GDP. The process has been documented by Jocelyn Bourgon (2009), Canada's Clerk of the Privy Council from 1994 to 1999. In launching the review, the prime minister presented the initiative to the Cabinet to emphasize its importance and later moved in lock-step with his Finance Minister, Paul Martin, in rejecting individual ministers' appeals for relief from spending targets. Across-the-board cuts were rejected, and the process relied instead on an evaluation of the relative importance of programs and services within the overall fiscal plan. At the departmental level, ministers and their deputy ministers were jointly accountable for delivery. A common set of principles for the review focused on the purpose of the program, its effectiveness, and affordability:

1. Does the program or activity continue to serve a public interest?
2. Is there a legitimate and necessary role for government in this program area or activity?
3. Is the current role of the federal government appropriate or is the program a candidate for realignment with the provinces?
4. What activities or programs should or could be transferred in whole or in part to the private or voluntary sector?
5. If the program or activity continues, how could its efficiency be improved?
6. Is the resultant package of programs and activities affordable within the fiscal restraint? If not, what programs or activities should be abandoned? (2009, 15)

Given the emphasis of three of the six review principles on alternative approaches to delivery, it is not surprising that decisions were made to transfer some government business to other sectors or to discontinue them entirely. Alternative Service Delivery (ASD) models were developed for national parks, food inspection, and revenue collection. Perhaps foreshadowing Paul Martin's later interest in social enterprises, the government also looked for partnerships with provinces, local communities, the private sector, and the not-for-profit sector to improve programs and services to citizens in areas such as youth job creation, tourism, freshwater fisheries management, environmental management, food safety, refugee settlement, and crime prevention. Some social programs were downloaded to provinces and territories, the federal government started to ease out of providing support for job training, and the provinces were offered the opportunity to take over the management of social housing (2009, 22). The program review, together with a favourable economic environment, the impact of some previous reforms, and growth in revenues resulting from tax reforms, saw the Canadian government wiping out its deficit three years later in 1997-98. This was followed by eleven consecutive years of budget surpluses.

Driving down deficits is one thing, but maintaining fiscal balance is another. When Conservative Prime Minister Stephen Harper took office in 2006 the books were still balanced, but two years later deficits returned, ballooning to over $55 billion in 2009, partly as a result of stimulus spending after the 2008 economic crisis. Annual deficits have continued since then, but had come down to $16.6 billion by 2014, with a balanced budget being declared in the 2015 budget.

Bourgon offers several lessons from the Program Review exercise. She notes that given its breadth as a "societal project", a major program review requires a more open and inclusive approach that engages the "whole of government." Similarly, in view of its scale, the project permitted a balancing of "single interests and collective interests." Bourgon also cautions against "easy cuts and easy targets", noting that these might not be sustainable and could undermine the capacity of government to achieve priority objectives. She advocates instead for ambitious reforms in which choices are made in a principled and defensible way from the perspective of citizens and public servants (2009, 24). She warns that efficiency measures based on "doing more for less" are insufficient to tackle sizeable deficits without a review and assessment of the relative importance of government programs (2009, 12-13).

This is an important story and I have seen many facets of it first-hand. In my previous role as a senior manager in Ontario's public service I was involved in several government-wide program review projects, under a variety of political administrations. Some involved blunt-instrument across-the-board cuts while others were thoughtful policy-based reviews, which made an effort to protect high-value programs while reducing or shedding those that were redundant, duplicative or of low value. In the mid-1990s, a 33 per cent across-the-board cut was made to the budgets of regulatory ministries as part of an overall 25 per cent cut in staff in Ontario's public service. As an assistant deputy minister I sat with colleagues around a boardroom table to work out how to implement this in our ministry. The easiest approach would have involved spreading the cut evenly across all departments but we knew this made little sense. It was obvious that some programs were more important than others and this led to some very tough decisions to completely close down or sharply reduce some programs in order to protect core programs that were of high value to ministry clients. Looking back twenty years, we had used a form of client focused approach in the downstream implementation of an across-the-board spending cut. As long as our budget was cut by 33 per cent, the government had no interest in how that was achieved, but we certainly did. Another medium-sized regulatory ministry elected to spread its cuts relatively evenly across the organization resulting in the loss of some critical mass of staff and expertise in key areas of its mandate. This had an impact on the quality of the ministry's ability to develop and implement policy for many years following. I tell this story because it reflects the often practical, middle ground that is available in the practice of public administration as well as the room for movement that public service leaders can sometimes find in the context of seemingly rigid political direction. I explore this more in Chapter 8 on public sector leadership.

Similarly, I have been involved in government-wide program review exercises in which a policy-based or "public value" assessment was used to generate proposals to the provincial Cabinet. In many of these cases there was nervousness at the political level about negative stakeholder and community (as well as regional or riding level) reactions to low value programs being cut. I have seen politicians of every political stripe blink when faced with the prospect of a political backlash – even though many of the proposals before them were clearly in the broader public interest. As a result, there is sometimes a leaning among the more risk-averse cabinet ministers towards evenly-spread cuts which "share the pain" because this is an easier political route. In these cases, the success of more targeted strategies relies on tight relationships between prime ministers or premiers and their respective finance ministers and heads of treasury boards, as well as convincing risk mitigation strategies.

Three instructive reports on approaches to deficit reduction are summarized below.

THE DRUMMOND REPORT

In 2011, the government of Ontario announced it would eliminate the province's $16 billion deficit by 2017. It asked Don Drummond, former Senior Vice President and Chief Economist at the Toronto Dominion (TD) Bank, to chair a Commission tasked with devising how this could be done without compromising important public services. The Commission's sophisticated and ground-breaking response, the 2012 *Report of the Commission on Reform of Ontario's Public Services* ("the Drummond Report"), is by far the most comprehensive study to date on the process of reforming Canadian public services in the context of a deficit, and offers over 360 recommendations for a path to fiscal balance and for reform of public services in Ontario (2012). The report goes further than others in offering some illustrative examples of substantive reforms in some of the largest and most expensive sectors such as health, education and social services.

Drummond started by challenging the government's own budget assumptions for a path to fiscal balance through its "2011 Budget scenario". Drummond provided an alternative "status quo scenario" based on his view of more realistic revenue and spending projections which suggested that, without program intervention, the deficit would double to $30.2 billion by 2017-18. The more challenging part of Drummond's task was in recommending how the government could sharply reduce government spending while sustaining or even improving critical public services. Drummond's starting point was that public services are not designed or delivered as effectively as they should be. His view is that improving public services and providing better value for money should always be a priority, even in the absence of big deficits. Drummond's advice, which included a blunt list of "do's" and "don'ts", (2012, 12) emphasized the importance of:

- Avoiding across-the-board spending cuts, focusing instead on protecting and improving high priority public services. This requires defining which businesses and services government should be involved in, and what policy goals and delivery mechanisms provide the best pathways to achieve those goals;

- Breaking down policy and delivery silos to provide more integrated approaches to service delivery;

- Standardizing services to citizens where it makes sense to do so, and specialize services where necessary. For example, it might make sense to standardize transactional back office functions such as purchasing, as well as high-volume routine medical procedures, while at the same time taking a customized approach to complex surgeries and supporting special needs children and seniors;

- Maximizing digitization for information management, client records and the delivery of online services, health diagnostics, and some health care delivery;

- Acknowledging that while government is an important funder, guarantor, and quality manager of services, it is not necessarily best at all forms of delivery. This means opening up the possibility of shifting more delivery to other levels of government, not-for-profit entities, and social enterprises, and in some cases the private sector. Drummond notes in his report that policy-making should be more porous as well, involving a broader range of stakeholders earlier in the process, including service users;

- Tackling the "web of rules" in which public sector organizations and public servants now operate (such as those governing access to social assistance and which preclude bundling siloed program funding to better serve clients with complex needs).

Many of these reform proposals are found in the report's sector-specific recommendations. Drummond focuses his attention on where the bulk of the budget is being spent. He notes that some of the biggest opportunities for improvement are in high cost sectors such as health, social services, education, and justice. These areas alone consume well over 80 per cent of the provincial budget. Drummond devotes lengthy chapters to each of these sectors, outlining substantial opportunities for reform with a focus on using evidence to support decision-making. In each case he describes key aspects of the current system and provides examples of the potential characteristics of a reformed system. The health chapter alone weighs in at fifty-seven pages and has 105 recommendations, including reshaping health system governance with more power and funding decisions being delegated to Local Health Integration Networks (LHINs), which plan, integrate, and distribute provincial funding for public health care services at a regional level; diverting more patients from hospital to community or home care; freezing doctors' pay; and, broadening the scope of practice for health professionals (Drummond 2012, 19-27). This could be a stand-alone blueprint for reform of the health care system but, at a minimum, it stands as a provocative and helpful green paper for much-needed reforms and, as of mid-2015, the Liberal government in Ontario was following many elements of that advice.

Drummond recommended similar approaches for education, justice, social services, employment and training, and other sectors. In the education sector, Drummond recommended scrapping (or at least delaying) implementation of the government's commitment to full day kindergarten, which at maturity would cost in the range of $1.5 billion per year. He also recommended increasing class size in elementary schools from an average of 20 students to an average of 23, noting that there is no causal connection between class size and student outcomes (2012, 29). Both of these changes, which were flagship political initiatives, were rejected by the government, although it has moved on many others.

Finally, on labour issues, Drummond notes that wages and benefits represent about half of all public sector program costs in Ontario, and that it is hard to envisage restricting overall annual spending growth to the desired 0.8 per cent if compensation costs rise faster than that. But he brings an interesting sense of perspective to this, avoiding draconian language and recommendations. He recommends that government should provide a zero budget increase for wage costs, in order to force efficiencies as offsets for any increases. In his mind, precedence should be given to hard-nosed collective bargaining, change-resistant "bumping" provisions and making some adjustments in the arbitration system. He recommends consolidation of the small bargaining units in the public sector to enable more standardization of working conditions and to help in finding efficiencies. Again, the government has followed much of this advice.

Recurring areas of focus in Drummond's recommendations are: assigning priority to programs and activities that invest in the future as opposed to the status quo; the promotion of a more evidence-based and porous approach to policy development and public service; and, seeking common themes across reforms to obtain economies of scale by reforming service delivery models and consolidating back office operations. Drummond emphasizes three critical success factors for successful reforms: the objectives and desired outcomes of the initiative must be clearly explained; the reforms should make sense to citizens, politicians, and public servants; and, the necessary processes and capacity must be in place to deliver desired outcomes (2012, 14).

There was a mixed response to Drummond's report. Social justice advocates argued that the report's focus on austerity will have negative implications for the most vulnerable Ontarians, while the political Opposition argued that the government is ignoring much of Drummond's advice. The government has reported that 60 per cent of the recommendations are being implemented, nine have been rejected, and the balance are being studied (Ontario Budget 2013).[11] In his own assessment of implementation in May 2013, Drummond offered the government a passing grade, noting that spending growth was in line with that recommended by the Commission (Globe and Mail 2013).

In commissioning the report, the government likely got more than it bargained for by way of advice on both its fiscal assumptions and recommendations directed at its flagship priorities. On the other hand, the report prompted significant media attention and political debate, which in turn highlighted the nature of the fiscal deficit and some issues and choices associated for public attention. As a broader "road map" for public service reform the report has contextualized labour costs as one element in a mix of recommended strategies, which in Drummond's mind should include a comprehensive review of programs and some consideration of options for additional revenue generation (2012, 411-27). Ontario's premier Kathleen Wynne announced in May 2015 that a partial divestment of Hydro One, the provincial electricity transmission and distribution company, is being considered, with a commitment that the proceeds of any sale would be committed to renewing provincial highway and public transit infrastructure,

Also building on Drummond's advice, a program review exercise was launched by Treasury Board President Deb Matthews early in 2015, alongside a pre-existing wage freeze policy. A government announcement said, "opportunities will be identified to improve services and outcomes based on measurable results, to ensure that sustained funding goes to initiatives that work. At the same time, the government will also have to make tough choices about services that are not performing, do not link to government priorities, or no longer serve a clear public interest."[12]

MOWAT'S SHIFTING GEARS STUDY

In 2010, the Mowat Centre at the University of Toronto's School of Public Policy and Governance partnered with consulting firm KPMG to produce *Shifting Gears: Paths to Fiscal Sustainability in Canada* (Mendelsohn et al. 2010). The study compares Canadian experience with efforts to improve fiscal balance with that of OECD countries. It makes a strong case for transformative approaches to deficit reduction and suggests several high-value opportunity areas for consideration by leaders. The starting point of the report is that traditional approaches to deficit reduction such as across the board spending and staffing cuts might be necessary elements of a deficit reduc-

The report recommends that governments focus on approaches that provide the best opportunities to effect long-term transformation of government programs, and where the financial dividends are significant.

tion strategy in the short term, but will not be transformative or lead to fiscal sustainability over the long term. The report argues instead that the current fiscal crisis provides governments with an opportunity to examine options through a "transformative lens."

The Mowat report identifies three broad approaches to deficit reduction: increasing revenues, cutting program spending through either targeted or across-the-board approaches, or re-examining how governments design and deliver public services. This latter approach includes "modernizing" government operations through new governance relationships and new financing mechanisms, and by adopting technologies and providing citizens with more choice in the ways they can access public services.

The report recommends that governments focus on approaches that provide the best opportunities to effect long-term transformation of government programs, and where the financial dividends are significant. It notes that governments across the political spectrum are examining these transformative models and hence they are not associated with a particular political philosophy. Echoing points made above, the Mowat report emphasizes the importance of political will and public acceptance as key preconditions for success. It, too, touches on internal capacity and processes, noting the importance of institutional structures that enable changes to be driven through complex, organizational, social and economic systems. In contrast to the Institute for Government study discussed below, which emphasizes the challenge of driving change from the centre of a strong unitary government, there is evidence in the Mowat paper of the opportunities and challenges in working across jurisdictional boundaries in a federal system of government.

The Mowat paper identifies a number of transformative approaches to deficit reduction that are consistent with trends in some other jurisdictions:

- Rationalizing tax collection (i.e., integrating national and sub-national sales taxes or consolidating or delegating to a single level of government tax filing, collections, and audit functions, both of which have been done in Canada). Carbon taxes of the sort in place in British Columbia and Australia's Mineral Resources Tax are further examples of transformative measures;

- Longer term embedded compensation reforms such as raising the retirement age or increasing the length of service required to trigger a public sector pension. This is one of the central tools being used in OECD countries, and Canada introduced a budget initiative in 2012 that will see the age for pension eligibility move from 65 to 67 years;

- Broadening "program review" exercises to encompass a "whole of system" approach and increase harmonization across levels of government (and presumably other sectors). Canadian examples include the delegation of immigration settlement services from the Canadian federal government to the province of British Columbia commencing in 1998, and a 2004 agreement between the federal government and the province of Ontario to harmonize and streamline parallel environmental protection reviews;

- Exploiting digitization to transform how individuals access public services. Approaches include putting services online to provide 24-hour access while reducing transaction costs; providing information to inform choices about providers (e.g., health wait times in Ontario); providing access to government data for use and re-use (e.g., Data.gov.uk); and enabling more inclusive approaches to developing policy, such as online budget processes in Cologne and Calgary;

- Modernizing public service processes through consolidation and the delegation of non-core functions to other providers. ServiceOntario in Canada and Australia's Centrelink are leading examples of modern and customer-focused service delivery models. David Varney has proposed a similar approach for UK back office consolidations, which have occurred at the sub-national level in Canada, and in August 2011 the federal government announced the creation of Shared Services Canada (2014). A similar approach has been recommended for the UK (Gershon 2004);

- Moving from direct government service delivery models to one that involves networks of government agencies, not-for-profit, and charitable organizations. These are becoming more common in Canada, particularly in the area of employment services. The Employment Program of British Columbia is a good example (Ministry of Social Development and Social Innovation 2014).

The Mowat report advocates a major focus on the areas of highest spending, especially where this spending is growing rapidly. In the case of health care spending this often involves large fiscal transfers to broader public sector institutions. Looking for reform opportunities where the big money is being spent makes obvious sense, but in many jurisdictions it is often the last place that political leaders choose to go because these tend to be areas of greatest concern to citizens: health, education, and social services – and in the case of more conservative jurisdictions – crime and justice.

The report makes a concluding effort to map its several large approaches to transformational reforms against four success criteria: public appetite, institutional capacity, overall effectiveness (in terms of fiscal outcomes), and transformational capacity (Mendelsohn et al. 2010, 44).

UNDERTAKING A FISCAL CONSOLIDATION – THE UNITED KINGDOM

In 2009, the UK-based Institute for Government developed an advisory paper on "Undertaking a Fiscal Consolidation" (McCrae, Myers and Glatzel 2009). The goal was to provide key information to politicians and officials involved in tackling the UK's fiscal challenges, which in 2009 saw two-thirds of its fiscal gap driven by high-cost sectors such as health and education in the context of a shrinking economy (2009, 3). The study was informed by a series of high-level seminars run by the Institute throughout 2009, discussions with senior policy-makers in the UK and abroad, and a review of the burgeoning relevant literature. The core of its advice centres on building a credible plan for deficit reduction and what the broad content of such a plan might include.

The paper identifies key success factors for government, touches on the relationship between the UK's centralized power in relation to local public service delivery, and discusses the challenge of departmental silos. It also considers the importance of timing – both in relation to electoral cycles, and in terms of the tension between a need for rapid fiscal relief and the longer term investments required to get ahead of known future pressures. It too, points to the importance of explicitly involving the public in understanding the major fiscal challenges and the choices available to deal with them.

It too, points to the importance of explicitly involving the public in understanding the major fiscal challenges and the choices available to deal with them.

A starting point for the IFG is the importance of tackling institutional inertia: how to build momentum and manage change. Political commitment, cabinet collegiality, and speed of implementation are also considered important. The study warns that plans that extend out over a long period face the risk of change fatigue, a sustained disruption to public services, and a negative impact on staff morale. On the other hand, moving too quickly also carries the risk of not putting in place sustainable plans. "Overall, there is likely to be an inverted U-shape between the timing and effectiveness of consolidations, with a representative study finding that sustained consolidations on average lasted around two to three years" (2009, 8).

The study places more emphasis than its Canadian counterparts on the importance of stronger local accountability for planning and delivery, as well as assuming more control over spending decisions (2009, 2). Commenting on successful approaches to deficit reduction in Canada, Sweden, and New Zealand , the IFG notes that while the nature of fiscal pressures differed, each country undertook comprehensive strategic reviews, which resulted in balanced budgets and improved economic performance.

In terms of key success factors, the IFG emphasizes the importance of transparency in explaining and reporting on reform initiatives but acknowledges that this reinforces a bias towards quick and demonstrable savings (such as reductions in benefit programs), which are easy to cost and result in immediate "cashable" savings. The same is true of compensation freezes, which can be put in the "front window" quite easily and are seen as politically advantageous. The more creative, transformative, and longer-term that initiatives are, the more important it is to signal early and continued progress through credible evidence. This in turn speaks to the importance of establishing hard timelines, metrics, and real-time data sources.

> **The more creative, transformative, and longer-term that initiatives are, the more important it is to signal early and continued progress through credible evidence.**

A second category of savings measures are less direct and in some cases incur some upfront costs, for example, reducing the role of government by curtailing activities or stopping them altogether; staffing cuts, which incur redundancy costs but are seen as important in demonstrating that pain is being shared across the public sector; and efficiency savings, which include a move to shared services and the consolidation of IT resources, real estate, and purchasing. Governments also controls fiscal transfers to other levels of government, thereby recording reductions in their own spending while leaving decisions about program reductions and/or revenue increases in the hands of others.

The IFG study concludes by discussing the difficult challenge of silos, which are particularly entrenched in the centralized architecture of Whitehall. This is contrasted with the perceived relative ease with which state or provincial levels drive innovation by realizing synergies across service delivery silos (2009, 12). The IFG points out that one of the most important opportunities for innovation and cost reduction lies at the local or municipal government level. This involves ensuring that local spending is rationalized both within and between service silos. At the very least, this should involve rapid adoption of the lessons emerging from the Total Place/Community Budgets initiatives discussed in Chapter 7. This initiative looks at how a "place-based" approach to public services can lead to better services at lower cost. It seeks to identify and avoid overlap and duplication between organizations, delivering a step change in both service improvement and efficiency at the local level, as well as across Whitehall.

CONCLUSIONS

There is now extensive international experience with deficit reduction strategies ranging from simple across-the-board spending cuts through to a sophisticated mix of government-wide and sector-based strategies driven by political and/or public priorities. This chapter has focused on policy-based or transformational deficit reduction strategies, which intersect with the reform and modernization of public services.

The three studies reviewed above are indicative of a shift in the policy discourse associated with fiscal restraint in Canada and the UK. These studies emphasize the importance of establishing a public conversation on the need for reforms, establishing a process for assessing the relative value of government programs and services, and carefully examining the areas of highest spending. The studies also point to opportunities to sustain, and possibly improve, public services that are most important to citizens. They speak in various ways about the importance of moving outside of departmental, ministry, and jurisdictional boundaries in the search for improvements in efficiency and quality. This is particularly the case in federal jurisdictions such as Canada, the United States, and Australia, where jurisdictional silos are piled on top of those built into the ministry-based architecture of Westminster models of government. Greater integration and collaboration figure heavily in Drummond's recommendations on both health system reform and the rationalization of duplicative federal, provincial, and municipal programs.

Drummond's work is particularly noteworthy. He artfully describes the challenges and opportunities and provides a sophisticated road map for reform. Many public service leaders and managers will understand precisely where Drummond is heading and will see significant opportunities to reshape policies, programs, and the way they are delivered. Drummond's advice on the importance of public education and dialogue on fiscal challenges is particularly important, as is his focus on bringing evidence to bear in the evaluation of policies and programs.

ADVICE FOR GOVERNMENTS, LEADERS AND PRACTITIONERS

- Top-level political and public service leaders must make some difficult decisions and present a vision of a reformed public service to employees and key stakeholders. The Canadian Program Review model provides good guidance on architecture and process. As The Economist notes, "Signals from the top determine what is ultimately delivered by politicians and what is not ... Officials, ministers and party foot soldiers like to know what the boss wants. If the boss isn't sure, or doesn't want to say, the fog descends" (2012, 50);

- While public service leaders and managers should continually strive to find efficiencies, challenging budget conditions also present an opportunity for leaders to make positive change. Many managers and staff know what is wrong with legacy systems and what is necessary to change them; it is important they be engaged in program review processes;

- Caution must be taken against an over-reliance on across-the-board spending cuts in view of the often temporary impact of these measures. The IFG paper is realistic in noting that political expediency will likely result in some arbitrary actions. My own experience with such cuts is that there are sometimes opportunities to adopt policy-based approaches in downstream implementation;

- A Program Review is not a quick fix. It takes time to examine programs and especially those in the high-cost and high-impact areas of human services and justice services. Some quick wins are important to show momentum to credit rating agencies and the media, and as "lighthouse" examples for public servants of what is necessary and doable. Longer-term approaches should include a shift from spending on current consumption to upstream investments, for example in children's mental health. The integration of often-siloed policy-making and direct service delivery stand out as opportunities for cost savings and quality improvement. This is particularly so in the areas of health and human services;

- The purpose and nature of the reforms should be explained clearly and transparently, and must make sense to citizens and public servants, as well as to elected officials who might have been outside of the process of decision-making; and,

- There must be appropriate internal processes to deliver desired outcomes. Drummond outlines a potential structure and mandates for a committee of senior central agency officials, a premier's results table and the Treasury Board.

The studies discussed above emphasize that transformative approaches to deficit reduction involve some tough choices about priorities, assessing the value of government programs and services, and addressing inefficient ways of doing business. This is hard, complicated, and often contentious work, which partly explains why it has been avoided for so long.

The key message for governments and public service leaders is that no single approach to deficit reduction is likely to be successful, least of all one that relies on across-the-board spending cuts or compensation restraint.

CHAPTER 6
ALTERNATIVE SERVICE DELIVERY

This chapter[13] provides an overview of Alternative Service Delivery (ASD). Common approaches to ASD involve the transfer of public services to private sector delivery agents and where public infrastructure is financed with private sector funding. There is a growing array of additional ASD models including Alliance Contracts, Public Service Mutuals and Social Impact Bonds (Hjartarson 2014, 33). ASD is often cited as a means to improving the efficiency and effectiveness of government programs, increasing value for money, and supporting institutional innovation (Drummond 2012). Public-Private Partnerships (P3), particularly in constructing transportation infrastructure, have been interwoven with the country's history and Canada continues to be a leader in this activity (The Conference Board of Canada 2013).

ASD has its roots in the New Public Management movement, which gained prominence in the 1980s. From the outset, ASD has been contested by public sector unions concerned about public sector jobs moving to private for-profit employers with less security, pay and benefits. Trade unions are opposed to public-private partnerships in principle, but are particularly concerned about the potential for new privately-financed facilities to be staffed by private sector workers. ASD has also been questioned by researchers comparing costs and benefits of public versus private sector delivery; inconclusive evidence continues to keep the debate alive and ASD is strongly contested (OPSEU 2014). This chapter reviews ASD's rise to prominence as part of the New Public Management movement, looking at the aggressive adoption of privatization and contracting out in the UK and at the state level in the US. Canada is then examined with a particular focus on the development of program review activities, the history and ongoing development of public-private partnerships, and experiences with competitive tendering or contracting out. The chapter concludes with a discussion of the contested nature of ASD.

ASD: ROOTS IN THE NEW PUBLIC MANAGEMENT

A powerful and enduring aspect of the New Public Management movement has been a move away from traditional bureaucracies and towards fragmented and semi-autonomous modes of service delivery, privatization, and a market-based approach to competitive contract tendering (Hood 1991; Aucoin 1995; Lynn 2006). Osborne and Gaebler (1993) popularized this shift by distinguishing between the role of governments in "steering" through policy-making and regulation as opposed to "rowing" in the sense of delivering public services which could be done in some cases by others. The contracting out of garbage collection in Phoenix, Arizona, in 1978, cited by Osborne and Gaebler (1993, 76-78) was offered as an example of a straightforward business-driven strategy transferred to the public sector.

Policies and practices falling under the rubric of this market-based approach to the organization of government services include: full-blown privatization; contracting out; public-private partnerships; and, more recently, social impact bonds and "asset recycling" (Fenn 2014). The driving forces behind this interest in a more competitive and disaggregated state include increasing global economic instability, a growing sense that post-war welfare states had become unaffordable; a loss of public confidence in government and the quality of public services; and an overriding belief in the virtues of private sector managerialism and efficiency (Peters and Waterman 1982; Pollitt and Bouckaert 2011, 6-8; Osborne 2010, 2). The enduring nature of this shift in thinking about the role of government has been matched by its adoption by political leaders across the political spectrum. Interest in privatization and contracting-out has remained stable across the political spectrum in both the UK and the US.

Until the 1970s, it was assumed that government held a natural monopoly on public service delivery, and in many cases it truly was the only game in town. There were very few alternative providers. As the scope of government services grew with the birth of the post-war welfare state, so did the size of government and the number of public servants at the federal and provincial levels. Governments grew to become some of the largest employers in the country, as they still are today. This was paralleled by similar growth in other sectors – the growth of national and multinational corporations were part of a burgeoning post-war bureaucracy throughout western democracies. The economy was growing and public sector growth did not stand out as being unusual.

In the context of the economic turbulence of the 1970s and early '80s with oil price shocks, runaway inflation, and the rise of fiscal deficits, manufacturers were forced to downsize, innovate, and relocate in the face of growing foreign competition – a change that has become permanent in the private sector. The public sector was at first shielded from the turbulence in the economy, a hiatus that saw significant growth in public sector unionization. Two massive shifts on either side of the Atlantic changed this in a hurry.

In 1979, Margaret Thatcher was elected as UK prime minister and promised to make Britain great again by getting its economic house in order, partially by curbing trade union power. This meant an end to government service monopoly and a shift to a smaller and more cost-effective government that was more responsive to citizens.

Thatcher set in motion an unprecedented wave of privatization, contracting out, and restructuring that changed the shape and nature of public services. Publicly-owned enterprises in coal, iron and steel, gas, electricity, water supply, railways, trucking, airlines, and telecommunications were privatized, along with public housing. Legislation required that the delivery of many other publicly-funded services should be subjected to compulsory competitive tendering. This mixed public-private model of delivery has continued under successive Conservative and New Labour governments, albeit with different labels. Tony Blair's Labour government passed legislation requiring local councils to take a "Best Value" approach in commissioning for garbage collection – a market-based approach that left the door open to extensive private delivery. In the 2010 election, Blair's Labour successor Prime Minister Gordon Brown's platform on public services was almost indistinguishable from that of the current Conservative Prime Minister David Cameron.

Today in the UK, private hospitals deliver private healthcare alongside publicly funded care, and "free schools", funded by government but run by parents' groups and charities (similar to North American "charter schools"), co-exist alongside traditional state schools. Policing is now supplemented by significant numbers of community volunteers, and private providers are bidding on a new Works Program targeted at the long-term unemployed that will pay for outcomes rather than inputs. In other words, payments to providers will be based on the verified employment of clients as opposed to the number counselled or retrained.

This intensification of private delivery was paralleled in the United States. In 1978, Proposition 13 or the "People's Initiative to Limit Property Taxation" was approved in California. This is regarded as part of the American taxpayer revolt that swept Ronald Reagan to the presidency in 1980. Proposition 13 also required a two-thirds majority of legislators to approve increases in State taxes. Similar to today's Tea Party slogan, "Hands off my Medicaid", the taxpayer revolt was not accompanied by reduced expectations about government services and entitlements. With revenues tightly squeezed, the tide turned against public sector workers and public sector service delivery with a vengeance. As in the UK, this resulted in a significant reshaping of the public sector with widespread contracting out of public services for private sector delivery.

These dramatic shifts in the UK and America were, and continue to be, underpinned by the belief that government monopolies are by nature bloated, inefficient, and undermined by the absence of competition. Critics reckoned that government had lost sight of its "core" business, and that public services would be better provided by private operators. Or, at the very least, that private sector business practices should be adopted by public service managers.

Osborne and Gaebler (1993) made a compelling case for a shake-up of public sector organizations and offered plenty of evidence on how and where this had already been done successfully. It has had a widespread impact on political leaders, including Tony Blair and Bill Clinton. Osborne and Gaebler also discussed breaking down government monopolies, focusing on customers' needs as opposed to government plans, and the potential for more decentralized and integrated forms of government. Some or all of these elements can be found in every public service reform plan in just about any democratic jurisdiction.

More recently the public versus private service dichotomy has become increasingly blurred by the myriad of hybridized organizational structures (such as state-owned enterprises) and professional services (such as those provided by medical doctors in countries with publicly funded medicare systems. Deber (2002) distinguishes between services that are publicly funded and the mix of options for their delivery, and emphasizes that private delivery is not a homogeneous category. Non-government providers can be not-for-profit or for-profit, with the for-profit category ranging from small businesses such as physicians' offices to corporate organizations, which are expected to provide returns on investment to their shareholders. Although approximately 70 per cent of Canadian health care is financed publicly, almost all of this care is already delivered by private (usually not-for-profit) providers. Thus comparisons between different types of delivery can be difficult since for-profit providers will often focus on the more profitable services and clients (2002).

ALTERNATIVE SERVICE DELIVERY IN CANADA

Canada has considerable experience with public service reform and its governments at all levels have experimented in varying degrees with privatization, public-private partnerships and contracting out. Canadian experience is reviewed below.

PRIVATIZATION

Privatization involves a permanent transfer of assets to private sector owners, often with ongoing government regulation. This commonly involves the sale of large-scale enterprises such as power generation companies, water treatment plants, and government-run transportation services. Large-scale privatization has not been prevalent in Canada, partly because of its limited degree of nationalization in comparison to countries such as the UK. Notable examples of privatization in Canada are the dispositions of Air Canada in 1988, Petro-Canada in 1991, and Canadian National Railways in 1995. There is an ongoing debate at provincial and municipal levels about the potential sale or "monetization" of electricity production and distribution companies under which up-front "balloon" payments are made to public sector owners in return for a consistent stream of revenues paid to private investors. There is a high degree of interest in these assets from large public sector pension funds in view of their interest in predictable income streams. For the same reason, there is widespread public and trade union concern about the implications of losing significant long-term revenue streams associated with public infra-structure. This discussion was relaunched in Ontario early in 2015 when the government announced that it was examining the possibility of divest-ing a part of its ownership of the Hydro One transmission and distribution company.

Alongside limited forays into privatization, Canadian governments have experimented widely with special operating agencies. These are large opera-tional or "rowing" functions transferred from government departments to arm's-length agencies, which are designed to operate more along the lines of a private undertaking. The Canada Revenue Agency, Canada Post Corporation, and provincial lottery and gaming agencies are prime examples, but they are far from private.

PUBLIC-PRIVATE PARTNERSHIPS

The UK and Australia were the first jurisdictions to experiment broadly with Public-Private Partnerships (P3) but have since been overtaken by Canada, which is now considered a leader in this field. P3s focus on generating private sector investment and expertise to support large public infrastructure proj-ects, commonly where there is perceived to be an "infrastructure deficit", such as with highways, mass transit, hospitals, university buildings, court facilities, and water, drainage, and sewage treatment plants. Proponents of P3s main-tain that, as well as bringing expertise and money, private sector involvement boosts efficiency, provides gains from time and cost certainty, involves more advance planning, and transfers a considerable degree of public sector risk to private sector partners. For example, unlike traditional financing arrange-ments under which constructors are paid monthly, P3 schemes see some or all payments held back until construction has been completed (The Conference Board of Canada 2013, 13). Value for money studies of P3s are reported to show average cost savings of 13 per cent compared with traditional public sector procurements (2013, ii). Ten to fifteen major P3s have reached financial close in Canada each year between 2007 and 2011 (2013, 7).

P3 development in Canada is found predominantly at the provincial level. Alberta, British Columbia, Ontario and Québec are leaders, partly due to their development of central procurement processes (2013, 5). British Columbia and Ontario are seen as the national pacesetters due to their development of purpose-built and well-resourced infrastructure organizations. Both have focused predominantly on health care, court facilities and highway/transit infrastructure. In Ontario alone, Infrastructure Ontario (IO) saw twenty-seven major P3 projects completed and in operation between 2004 and 2013, with a further nineteen projects scheduled for completion by 2015 (2013, 54-59). A 2014 study by the Altus group reported that 97 per cent of these projects were delivered within the IO managed budgets, and 72 per cent have achieved substantial completion within one month of the scheduled dates.[14]

P3s can involve design only, or both design and construction, and can also include maintenance and, potentially, the operations of the new structures.

At the federal level, the government of Canada established a $1.25 billion P3 fund in 2007 and also created a P3 office, which has since evolved into PPP Canada.

P3s can involve design only, or both design and construction, and can also include maintenance and, potentially, the operations of the new structures. In Canada, ownership of facilities constructed under P3 arrangements generally remain in public hands or revert to full public ownership once a negotiated lease or concession expires. This approach skirts the controversy associated with outright privatization, particularly where hot-button institutions such as health care facilities are involved. In Ontario, up-front guarantees have been provided that new facilities will be staffed by public sector workers. Elsewhere, a water filtration plant built in Moncton, New Brunswick in 1999 under a P3 arrangement that was later privatized under a lease-buy arrangement has attracted significant controversy (Kalen-Sukra 2012). Ontario's early experiments with P3s in the health sector were not without difficulties. Significant cost overruns attracted scrutiny and then criticism from the province's Auditor General (OPSEU 2014). This learning prompted the government to develop its in-house capacity and move to a dedicated P3 organization, Infrastructure Ontario.[15] More recently, there has been a growing contrast in Ontario between performance improvements in projects managed by Infrastructure Ontario and those managed under traditional models by public sector departments and agencies, which continue to experience major cost overruns.

Risks associated with P3s include higher private borrowing costs, transaction costs and, in some cases, failure to effectively transfer risk to the private sector (The Conference Board of Canada 2013, ii). Vining and Boardman (2008) are sceptical about the efficacy of P3s as a widely replicable mechanism for delivering public infrastructure. But they acknowledge that P3s in Canada have worked in three types of circumstances: cases where governments have not attempted to transfer use or revenue risk to the private sector; where projects have required specialized knowledge or proprietary technology that is only held by private sector firms; and, where governments were able to transfer construction risk at something close to a fixed price.

A recurring theme in research is the importance of developing commercial capacity inside government (Vining and Boardman 2008; The Conference Board of Canada 2013; Gash et al. 2013). Notably, both British Columbia and Ontario have established dedicated secretariats with a mix of public and private sector experts in order to strengthen their capacity for business planning, risk assessment, deal making, and deal management.

CONTRACTING OUT

Contracting out or "competitive tendering" involves opening up work to competitive bidding. Canada has not been as aggressive in this area as the UK and New Zealand, and, unlike in those countries, there has been no legislative or prescriptive requirement from government. Consistent with many other countries, contracting out in Canada is common in food preparation and cleaning in public sector institutions such as hospitals and universities, waste management and water distribution at the municipal level, and highway maintenance at municipal and provincial levels.

Some provinces have moved beyond these areas. In Ontario, driver licence testing is contracted out to UK-based SERCO, which in its home country is also regularly hired to manage failing public schools. SERCO is one of a number of private sector companies which provide services to both public and private sector clients. The company is sophisticated and highly efficient; its core business is providing reliable contracted services. In 2013, British Columbia contracted out its employment support services to 74 community-based providers, which are partly funded on the basis of achieving measured outcomes. This integrated a number of services previously provided by multiple federal and provincial agencies and now connects the new centres with an integrated client case management system. This represents an early foray into the outsourcing of professional services provided directly to clients.

There is abundant literature on the benefits and downsides of contracting out. Advocates say that competition creates pressure for efficiency, cost reduction, and innovation, as well as adding specialist expertise, management, and monitoring of outcomes. Somewhat incorrectly, this is contrasted with perceptions of government as slow, inflexible, and wasteful, and more interested in self-preservation than in innovation.

Economists have had a field day figuring out the potential and actual savings of ASD. The data vary widely with most studies landing on savings of 15 to 20 per cent. But this is an area in which generalization is tricky and everything is contested. Outcomes are situational and vary considerably both within and between industries. Cost savings from contracting out are reported by some to range from 20 to 40 per cent with comparable or better service levels following contracting out (Savas 2000). Contradictory research finds that, with the possible exception of garbage collection and building cleaning, there is no evidence of private sector advantage in service delivery, or it finds that the results are mixed at best (Hodge 2000). Bel and Warner (2006) looked at forty years of econometric studies dealing with municipal waste collection and water distribution, finding that the majority of studies revealed no cost or efficiency advantage arising from private provision of these services. They point to reduced competition in these areas resulting from a "first mover" advantage when bids are reopened and increasing consolidation in the industries. Indeed, it is not uncommon for this to result in "reverse contracting" in which work that has been contracted out is taken back in-house.

UNION RESPONSES

Contracting out and privatization are incendiary issues for the trade union movement (OPSEU 2014). Labour critics say that competitive tendering often moves public sector work to non-union employers, drives down wages and benefits, and opens the door to corruption and bid rigging. Unions have made substantial efforts get prohibitions or expensive penalties into their agreements to deter the practice. The Canadian Union of Public Employees (CUPE) sees this as a life or death issue for their membership and this is reflected in local negotiations and central in its political agenda. A significant portion of CUPE's website is devoted to challenging privatization of government services. CUPE communications cite a 2010 Environics poll showing that 81 per cent of respondents trust the public sector more than the private sector to provide drinking water treatment and delivery.

Other studies tell a more complex story. An Ipsos Reid study commissioned by the Council for Public-Private Partnerships found that two-thirds of Canadians support the use of public-private arrangements to deliver infrastructure and a range of public services (Canadian Council for Public-Private Partnerships 2010). The highest levels of support for private involvements were in the construction and operation of public recreation facilities (74 per cent), the operation of non-health related services in public hospitals (73 per cent), and in the construction and maintenance of roads (72 per cent). The poll also found that more than half of unionized workers in the public sector support a public-private delivery mix. It further suggests a generational rift. Some 74 per cent of Canadians between the ages of 18-29 support more private involvement in service delivery, compared with just over 60 per cent support among Canadians aged sixty or older.

In the late 1990s, efforts by Premier Mike Harris's Conservative government in Ontario to aggressively pursue ASD were stiffly resisted by the Ontario Public Service Employees Union (OPSEU). In 1997, long and costly delays in plans to contract-out highway maintenance in Ontario led to greater government efforts to find jobs for affected OPSEU members. In some cases, expensive and time-consuming hearings at labour tribunals and in the courts can negate the benefits of contracting out. Effective union lobbying campaigns can raise public concern about loss of service quality and sour the employer's relationship with the balance of the government workforce – both of which have offsetting costs against the benefits of alternative delivery.

BUILDING CAPACITY FOR ASD

There is an increasing trend towards social and community services being provided by a mix of public providers and community-based not-for-profit agencies, social enterprises, and voluntary organizations. As the complexity of care increases, the intrinsic values and motivation found in public or not-for-profit delivery organizations might be better suited to meet individual client needs. In view of the benefits of increased cross-organizational collaboration required in this field, Sturgess (2012) has suggested that governments could play a more active and collaborative role in organizing and managing this market as a "public service economy". Recognizing the complications involved in outsourcing decisions, Farneti et al. (2010) have outlined a range of governance options that could be applied depending on the complexity of service delivery arrangements. In addition, Gash et al. (2013) and Hjartarson et al. (2014) have emphasized the importance of capacity building in government for all aspects of ASD.

In Canada, British Columbia established a dedicated ASD Secretariat in 2003, which by 2013 had coordinated ten large-scale, long-term ASD contracts with a total value of about $2.5 billion. These include the automation and processing of health insurance provider and BC PharmaCare payments, internal payroll services, and a multi-agency effort to extend and improve high-speed Internet services to rural and remote communities. Financial savings to government have been estimated at $550 million over ten years. The objectives of the secretariat included maintaining and enhancing service delivery, reducing costs and/or increasing revenue, transferring operating risk to the private sector, and benefitting from collaboration with the private sector. It assists in resolving cross-ministry issues, provides specialist expertise in deal-making, and brings commercial discipline to decision-making. Labour issues are managed up front in negotiations with the British Columbia Government Employees' Union. Where jobs are moved to an alternative service provider, the same or better benefits are offered together with retention of the pension plan and union membership (Hjartarson et al. 2014).

Key lessons arising from the secretariat's work include the importance of political and executive support, dedicated funding for the central units (essential for cross-government success), engaging proactively with stakeholders, breaking down silos and working proactively on a labour relations strategy (2011, 16).

DELEGATED ADMINISTRATIVE AUTHORITIES

In a different sphere, Ontario has been an innovator in moving some regulatory services to 'Delegated Administrative Authorities' (DAAs). There are nine such authorities in the province covering a broad range of activities, including electrical safety, the travel industry, and the provision of funeral services. The administrative authority assumes complete financial, operational and legal responsibility for administering legislation, which includes delivering day-to-day regulatory services such as licensing, inspections, prosecutions and fee setting. It is managed by an independent board of directors. The programs are fully cost recovered from the regulated businesses through licensing, inspection and other fees. Service delivery is cost neutral to government since the cost of government oversight is recovered through fees charged to the DAAs. The ministry retains overall accountability for the performance of the Administrative Authority, and control of the delegated legislation. The model applies a risk-based approach to compliance and enforcement and has piloted new ways to deliver services. Based on Ontario's experience the provinces of Alberta, British Columbia and Saskatchewan have created similar bodies.

CONCLUSIONS

Several key points can be drawn from research and practice in the area of alternative service delivery.

First, cost reductions and/or quality improvements are not guaranteed by the transfer of work to private sector providers. Similarly, P3s do not guarantee on time delivery or cost savings in relation to traditional procurement mechanisms. Achieving desired outcomes requires tight descriptions of performance expectations, a careful assessment of risk, rigorous monitoring and performance management. Even then, efficiencies may diminish over time as costs escalate or competition diminishes.

Second, activities that easily lend themselves to measurement and evaluation have been common candidates for contracting out. Examples include garbage collection, institutional food preparation, cleaning, laundry and some routine maintenance tasks. The same is true of routinized high-volume work such as laboratory testing and some aspects of home care in the health sector, payroll services and some lower-level human resources tasks (many employers have contracted out the initial processing and screening of job applicants to recruitment companies).

Third, the growing hybridization and complexity of modes of service delivery requires improved government capacity to organize and manage these arrangements (Gash et al. 2013; Hjartarson et al. 2014). This again points to the importance of high-level capacity and leadership in the field of human resources in public sector organizations.

Fourth, where government has developed strong internal capacity for commissioning and managing contracts thought could be given to experimentation with competition within and between levels of government (i.e., a purely "public sector" market).

Fifth, given the degree of trade union opposition to ASD arrangements, some of which has been quite successful (OPSEU 2014), very little research has been devoted to this dynamic. Hjartarson et al. (2014, 17), have touched on this in calling for governments to negotiate public sector employee transfer agreements that would outline the rights and obligation of the government, public sector workers, and service providers in ASD arrangements. They also recommend pension frameworks that would allow transferred public sector employees to maintain membership in public sector pension plans (2004, 28).

ADVICE FOR GOVERNMENTS, LEADERS AND PRACTITIONERS

- Experience in Canada and abroad suggests that building strong internal capacity for assessing and negotiating ASD arrangements is an important success factor. This should ideally be housed in a specialized central organization with dedicated funding. ASD organizations should develop capacity for:

  - Supporting organizational efficiency assessments;

  - Identifying and assessing candidates for ASD, as well as conducting additional assessments of the many programs that are not considered to be viable candidates for ASD (this latter capacity could be developed as part of a broader effort to strengthen organization-wide capacity for program evaluation);

  - Commercial and deal-making skills;

- Commissioning and managing services; and,

- Risk assessment and risk transfer.

- Governments should increase efforts to build relationships with, learn from, and collaborate with service providers and service users, with an emphasis on identifying challenges and opportunities in the design of public sector programs and services.

- The governance of service delivery networks is emerging as a critical factor, particularly as these arrangements bring together a broader range of delivery organizations from various sectors. A range of governance options are available depending on the complexity of the ASD models. The establishment of clear lines of accountability will be of particular interest to elected representatives. In view of emerging concepts of "mixed markets" and "public service economies", a key decision is the extent to which governments have an appetite to intervene in organizing and "stewarding" markets of service providers in order to ensure appropriate levels of collaboration between providers, close relationships with clients and a competitive marketplace. Such collaborations can be messy and unpredictable.

- Wherever possible, ASD partnerships should incorporate outcomes-based contracting. In the social, community and justice sectors consideration should also be given to joint commissioning where different departments are seeking related outcomes. For example, in the UK, the Department of Justice and Department of Work and Pensions are exploring a single outcomes-based contract for reoffending and employment outcomes (Blatchford and Gash 2012).

- In view of the complex and controversial labour issues associated with ASD proposals, early dialogue with unions is critical. Governments should consider the early negotiation of over-arching labour frameworks dealing with compensation, benefits and the retention of public sector pension plan and union membership.

The focus on privatization, P3s and contracting out has diverted attention from an entirely new frontier in service delivery. Jurisdictions like New Zealand and the UK are shifting the focus of social services, children's services and some justice services towards much more localized and community-sensitive service models. Previously siloed funding from multiple government departments and agencies is being consolidated and focused on addressing complex and expensive social challenges such as homelessness, domestic violence and long-term unemployment. This does not involve public versus private debates – it focuses on the needs of vulnerable adults and children and the broad range of health and social services necessary to respond to complex needs. The result is a collaborative mix of public, not-for-profit, private and community-based voluntary organizations as well as emerging social enterprises. Over the past several years there has been growing interest on the part of both the government of Canada and a number of provinces in supporting social enterprises as well as engaging in "social purchasing."[16]

CHAPTER 7
INTEGRATED SERVICE DELIVERY IN CANADA AND THE UNITED KINGDOM

INTRODUCTION

In response to challenges arising from the siloed architecture of governments, public service organizations in many countries have worked hard to build horizontal cultures, management skills and practices. This has been characterized as joined-up government or "integrated public governance" (Kernaghan 2009). The character of horizontal management at the federal level in Canada has been reviewed by Evert Lindquist (2002 and 2012) who regards a horizontal mind-set as a prerequisite for those working in the public sector (2002, 153). Within the broader scheme of building more horizontal and networked organizations, this chapter explores the shift over the past two decades towards integrating previously fragmented approaches to public service delivery. This shift is discussed at two levels: the integration of high-volume transactional services, such as the provision of birth certificates and driver's licences across front counters, and the more complex realm of integrating human services provided to clients, many of whom rely on multiple service providers.[17]

This development is a particularly important aspect of public service reform as it offers a tangible opportunity to improve service delivery to citizens at a comparable or lower cost (Seidle 1995). Particular attention is given to Canada's leading role in this area, especially in developing integrated back office, front counter and web-based service delivery. Canada is also a leader in measuring and benchmarking customer expectations in relation to various modes of service delivery and their reactions to service improvements. This is a mixed story however in the sense that while Canada's federal government has worked hard to develop a horizontal culture, it has also struggled somewhat since the mid-1990s to maintain momentum (Lindquist 2002 and 2012). Lessons are also drawn from Ontario's experience with service integration, which despite some challenges, has seen service integration grow and mature to the extent that it has been widely studied by a number of jurisdictions around the globe.

In keeping with the uneven and contextual nature of public service reforms (Pollitt and Bouckaert 2011), it is notable that while Canada is considerably ahead of the UK in the integration of high-volume over-the-counter transactional services, the UK is making greater strides in integrating human services in collaboration with local government organizations (Dean and Boutilier 2012).

Following a surge of interest in horizontal governance at the federal level in the late 1990s and early 2000s, Lindquist noted a drop-off in both research and the active pursuit of expanded horizontal initiatives, surmising that this was prompted by a more risk averse environment and the command and control style of the Conservative government which had been elected in 2006 (Lindquist 2012, 31-32).

Leslie Seidle (1995) has documented the genesis of integrated service delivery initiatives at the federal and provincial levels in Canada and offers an interesting perspective on British Columbia and Ontario's efforts in the 1980s and 1990s. Seidle reminds us that British Columbia's "Government Agents" model, which saw agents across the province delivering services on behalf of fifty programs, dates back to 1858 (1995, 118). Lindquist and White (1994) have also looked in-depth at earlier efforts at reform in Ontario over several decades.

MEASURING CITIZENS' EXPECTATIONS

Efforts to integrate fragmented public services are often described as being "customer driven" or "customer focused." This is a virtuous and sensible objective but is often undervalued in planning, implementation, and monitoring and measuring results. Canada's efforts to improve service delivery have been both supported and validated by sophisticated and rigorous benchmarking.

In 1999, an intergovernmental Citizen-Centred Service Network (CCSN) was created, composed of over 200 senior officials from the three levels of Canadian government together with academics and outside experts in public sector service delivery. The same year, the CCSN released a series of reports, tools, and recommendations aimed at improving citizen satisfaction with public sector service delivery.

"Citizens First" is a triennial national survey of Canadians' expectations, satisfaction levels and priorities for service improvement across three levels of government in Canada. The survey also measures citizens' satisfaction with public services against private sector services such as banks, supermarkets and department stores. It has found that citizens' expectations of public sector service quality match or exceed levels they expect from private companies. Another important finding is that high levels of service quality tends to drive higher levels of confidence in government. A "Common Measurement Tool" supports the survey. The tool is used by government departments in assessing client satisfaction and benchmarking performance within and between levels of government. Ralph Heintzman states that, "The Citizens First series … has established the gold-standard for research on public sector service delivery, not only in Canada, but around the world. The ICCS methodology and approach have equipped public sector managers with the tools they need to identify action priorities for service improvement" (Institute for Citizen-Centred Service 2008).

THE DIRECTION OF REFORM

Over the past three decades, public service organizations around the world have been responding to economic pressures and rising expectations on the part of citizens and political leaders. Under the populist label of "reinventing government" (Osborne and Gaebler 1993), the 1980s and 1990s saw many political leaders call for smaller, more customer-focused, competitive and integrated governments and public services.

Reforms have included experimentation with privatization and a focus on measurement, value for money, and an emphasis on outcomes rather than inputs. While some of these initiatives, such as privatization, have gained intermittent traction over time, the drive towards more "joined-up" or integrated government services has been relatively constant. Some form of integration, especially in relation to policy-making and service delivery, is now generally found at the core of national and sub-national modernization initiatives. The language of "joining up" of public services has become ubiquitous. Kenneth Kernaghan (2009, 239-54) has referred to this mode of reform as "Integrated Public Governance" and suggests that it may be the successor to the New Public Management.

In parallel with the shift towards integration, governments have made increasing efforts to become more "citizen focused" and thus attuned to citizens' needs and interests (Pollitt and Bouckaert 2011, 151-52). This trend has intensified in recent years as citizens have demanded the same or better services from government as those available in retail stores and on a 24/7 basis through the Internet. The result has been a shift towards "citizen-centred government", an implicit acknowledgement that governments might not know what is best for citizens and, potentially, a first step in rebuilding trust with an increasingly disenfranchised electorate (Aucoin 1995, 184).

In general, "joining up" is often implemented or is being planned in one or both of two areas:

> *"Transactional"services.* Common candidates for collabora-
> tion and integration in this category include: internal "back
> office" services such as payroll and benefits management,
> business management including billings and payments;
> high-volume human resources transactions; information
> technology; and, procurement. As ministries and depart-
> ments joined up their own services some looked outwards
> to the larger and more provident shift to the provision of
> direct services to citizens. This has involved the successful
> integration of front counter services in which one or more
> departments offer services across common counters (such
> as business registration, driver's licences, identity cards and
> parking permits) and through common websites or call
> centres, data sharing, and collaborative approaches to regu-
> lation. Service Canada and provincial counterparts such as
> Service BC, ServiceOntario and Service New Brunswick are
> obvious examples.

Integrating Human Services. The more complex, but growing, area of collaboration involves efforts to integrate health, community or justice services in ways that better serve complex needs clients. Interest in this area has been heightened in recent years as political leaders turn their attention to difficult or "wicked" policy and delivery issues such as poverty, children's services, mental health, homelessness, and the health and community care challenges associated with aging populations. Such challenges are not only complex, they are expensive and becoming more so. There is a growing fiscal imperative to find efficiencies together with a critical political imperative to maintain or improve current service levels.

The complexity in the field of human services flows in part from the need of many clients for a complex mix of health and social services and from the service relationships between providers and clients. There has been an explosion of interest in this around the world as health care costs have risen alongside greater demand for social and community services, especially those associated with children and the elderly. Researchers have made an effort to capture the complexity of these relationships with reference to network theory, which explores public management from the perspective of coordinating and managing networks of disparate actors engaged in policy-making and service delivery (Agranoff and Maguire 2003; Klijn 2005, 267-72). Central to this has been the deployment of a number of different strategies, including interventions into pre-existing networks, motivating participants towards a desired goal, and establishing coordinating mechanisms to maximize the value of interactions in achieving those goals (Koppenjan and Klijn 2004).

In the context of federal and quasi-federal jurisdictions, developing more integrated approaches to policy-making and service delivery involves cross-boundary collaboration both vertically and horizontally. Canada's extensive experience in all of these fields of service integration makes it possible to draw out lessons for practitioners and leaders.

Horizontal or intra-governmental integration and collaboration involves joining up some or all of these services within one level of government. These efforts usually focus on the economies of scale derived from collaborative approaches to procurement; the efficiencies and knowledge management advantages associated with developing common IT platforms; and merged front counter services with the associated benefits of consolidating real estate. In federal jurisdictions such as Canada and Australia, reforms are often incubated at the provincial and state level and evolve into national programs.

Vertical or intergovernmental integration sees two or more levels of government collaborating on joint service delivery initiatives, for example, Centrelink in Australia and 'Getting it Right for Every Child' in Scotland. These efforts have in some cases led to previously duplicated services being cross-delivered by a single level of government (for example, the Canadian federal government administers corporate taxes and/or sales taxes on behalf of several Canadian provinces).

If efforts to join up services across departments within one level of government are challenging, the project of joining up across levels of government is many times more complex. This is particularly the case where there is a misalignment of party politics or historical and/or constitutional barriers to joint service delivery (Dean and Boutilier 2012).

In a report prepared for the Ottawa-based Forum of Federations, Dean and Boutilier (2012) reported on the recent trajectory, progress and future plans of several federal jurisdictions engaged in working across jurisdictional boundaries to improve service delivery to citizens. For each country case study, descriptions were provided on the status and trajectory of integrated service delivery initiatives. The report focused on areas in which the United Kingdom, Canada, Australia and Germany are breaking new ground or are established leaders in one or more modes of service delivery. The balance of this chapter explores leading examples of joint initiatives involving transactional services, and more complex efforts to integrate front-line delivery of human services. Greater attention is paid to Canada's success in integrating transactional services, whereas the UK is referenced for leading examples of efforts to integrate human services or justice services in order to better tackle complex issues for vulnerable populations.

PART ONE: INTEGRATING TRANSACTIONAL SERVICE DELIVERY IN CANADA

The Canadian Constitution delineates the division of powers between the federal government, its ten provinces and three territories. Canada's federation is complex, interwoven with its development as a nation, and has made accommodations for cultural and linguistic differences. In this sense it reflects Alan Fenna's (2010, 9) description of federations that evolve "into highly complex and messy arrangements of political and administrative entanglement which conform only very approximately to ideal type models." Shifts in the economy, technological change, urbanization and changes in the role of the state have also resulted in overlap in the division of powers between the two levels of government.[18]

Canada has earned an international reputation for its success in developing a customer-focused and integrated approach to delivering transactional services.

Despite these complexities and ambiguities, which in many respects relate to funding as opposed to hands-on delivery of services, the constitutional division of powers (supported by judicial interpretations) in Canada is relatively clear in charging provinces and territories with the delivery of the lion's share of direct services to citizens. In turn, provinces and territories have devolved many areas of direct service delivery to municipalities.

Canada has earned an international reputation for its success in developing a customer-focused and integrated approach to delivering transactional services. It is regularly mentioned in international reports as a world leader in integrated service delivery, in particular through its federal service delivery brand, Service Canada (UK Cabinet Office 2009; Accenture 2007). Outside of periodic interest in public sector compensation and alternative service delivery, Canada's political leaders tend to take a back seat in most areas of public administration, perhaps seeing this as the domain of the public service. Thus, despite the important government-citizen interface implicit in service delivery, there has been very little political involvement in the conception, design or governance structures of integrated service initiatives. This has stayed in the hands of the public service. Nevertheless, it has obviously been important to obtain the support of political leaders, particularly where structural changes are contemplated and staff or clients in local political ridings might be affected by change initiatives. The key point here is that public service reform in Canada has not been seized as part of the political agenda. This is a mixed blessing. While there has been lots of latitude for public service leaders to innovate, this has not always received the appropriate support at the political level necessary to achieve substantial momentum (Aucoin 1995; Lindquist 2002 and 2012).

There are situations in which service delivery becomes a political issue, particularly where there are complaints about timeliness or quality. In Ontario, for example, in the aftermath of 9/11 more rigid requirements for identity documents intensified a pre-existing backlog in processing birth certificates – extending it to a nine-month wait on average. This was a significant challenge for a newly-elected provincial government as well as the public service that was making service quality a priority. In 2004, Ontario Premier Dalton McGuinty made it clear to the public service that he wanted this fixed. A team led by Deputy Minister Michelle DiEmanuele mapped the paper-based application and processing chain and concluded that moving the process online could reduce the processing time from months to days. In addition, per-unit processing costs would be reduced from dollars to cents. An important structural change arising from this initiative was the merging of the corporate HR and IT functions with the department charged with driving integrated approaches to service delivery. This recognized the importance of human resources leadership in major change processes and the role of information technology as an important business tool in supporting public service reform.

With approval from the premier and head of the public service the new model was put in place with the added mustard of a money-back service guarantee. In a switch from the previous flood of complaints, staff working in the birth certificate processing centre started receiving thank you notes commending them on the quick turnaround. These were pinned up on the office walls – and a lesson learned was that positive testimonials about public services that work well and please clients enhance public servants' motivation and morale. Moving this application to a digital mode of service delivery in the wake of the post- 9/11 emphasis on security was a risky proposition, but with a sufficient emphasis on identity validation, risk management and mitigation and careful piloting and testing, implementation went smoothly.

A 2012 report by Dean and Boutilier draws on qualitative data from Canadian key informants, reporting that high-level public service leadership is an important pre-condition for further progress in breaking down organizational and jurisdictional boundaries. Public service leadership has been a consistent thread in the Canadian service delivery experience, especially given fairly regular changes of governing party at the federal and sub-national levels. The

Public service leadership has been a consistent thread in the Canadian service delivery experience.

knowledge on the part of public servants that integrative reforms have been driven by public service leaders has likely been a sustaining success factor in the achievement of buy-in from managers and front-line service delivery staff.

Also of note is that Canada's federal government is to some extent a beneficiary of "laboratory federalism" (Fenna 2010), a term referring to the process by which national governments are provided with an opportunity to learn from the experience of sub-national governments' experimentation with policy and delivery. Canada's national government has been adept at monitoring, learning from, and adapting the experience of provincial incubators. This has been the case with the integration of service delivery. Provinces moved first in joining up siloed back office and front counter services within their own boundaries. In a second phase the federal government began to join up its front office services under the Service Canada brand. A third phase saw some larger provinces, such as Ontario and British Columbia, making the case for federal, provincial and municipal collaboration and co-location.

At the provincial level there has been a steady evolution over the past fifteen years in moving from disconnected ministry-specific front counters, websites and call centres and towards co-located common counters. This in turn required that back office services, including IT platforms, were developed to support merged front counter operations. In some cases (e.g., British Columbia and Ontario) this prompted thinking about enterprise-level approaches to other business lines such as billing, payroll administration, procurement and human resources.[19]

When counters and service offerings were consolidated, it became increasingly obvious that just as shared platforms were replacing ministry service silos, they could equally cross jurisdictional boundaries. Provincial officials realized that federal services such as the issuance of social insurance numbers and business registrations, and municipal services such as birth registration, should be added in order to offer a full suite of services. This contributed to enhanced provincial-federal-municipal partnerships, including broader online service bundling and the co-location of federal, provincial and municipal services behind common physical counters across the country. While provinces have incubated integrated service strategies, and to some extent encouraged federal involvement, a federal government strategy has now been developed and, as of 2015, is the subject of collaborative discussions between federal/provincial/territorial deputy ministers.

SERVICEONTARIO

ServiceOntario, which operates in Canada's most populous province of 13 million citizens, saw its genesis in the late 1990s, well in advance of the creation of Service Canada. Lindquist and White (1994) and Seidle (1995) have described the fledgling efforts that preceded this more comprehensive launch. The service organization has won numerous awards for its "outside-in" customer focused approach to integrated service delivery. It has combined the service offerings of more than a dozen ministry-based front counters, websites and call centres into unified ServiceOntario counters throughout the province. ServiceOntario was also the first Canadian jurisdiction to introduce a "money-back" service guarantee for a growing range of public services and to integrate online services on a large scale. "Despite the wide dispersion of its population, by 2010, close to 95 per cent of Ontarians were estimated to be within 10 kilometres of an integrated ServiceOntario centre" and more than 80 services are provided through nearly 1000 touch points (ServiceOntario 2011).

ServiceOntario also initiated some of the first significant integration efforts with the federal government and municipalities, such as the bundling of a one-time application for three services, previously only available from separate offices: municipal birth registration, provincial birth certificates and the federal Social Insurance Number. These are now available through a single online application process with a money-back service guarantee. New mothers are able to apply before leaving hospitals with their newborns.

To varying degrees, Canada's other provinces and territories are also innovators and leaders. Service New Brunswick continues to be cited as a leading service integrator (for example, its partnership with Service Canada on the issuance of boating licences), together with Nova Scotia and British Columbia.

ServiceOntario's achievements did not unfold easily, however, and were subject to many of the challenges identified in the literature dealing with horizontal integration such as turf protection on the part of public service and political officials (Seidle 1995; Lindquist 2002). By 2002, there had been some early momentum as smaller and cash-strapped ministries shifted their front counter responsibilities to the new organization. But it also became clear that, with just over 50 per cent of front counter services transferred to ServiceOntario common counters, the initiative was slowing down. Governance challenges resulting from an initial decision to delegate leadership of ServiceOntario to a line ministry, as well as an understanding that ministries could transfer their counter services at their own pace, and on a voluntary basis, were taking a toll. Larger and more muscular ministries with high volumes of service transactions were a tougher sell. And yet the inclusion of the larger ministries were important in moving the new integrated services organization to critical mass and a point of organizational no return. In some cases, senior ministry officials and ministers offices were concerned that their ministry would be losing control of the levers that impact service quality while retaining accountability for the same services if something went wrong. In other cases the concern was just about losing turf.

In 2002, following my appointment as Cabinet Secretary and head of Ontario's public service I initiated my own size-up of the organization. I had been under the impression that ServiceOntario had achieved critical mass since it seemed that victory had already been declared. Given the importance of integrated service delivery from a client perspective and my own concerns about the inefficiencies associated with silos in government this seemed like an obvious and natural first leadership priority. I assumed that I could simply ask that the recalcitrant ministries join their counterparts in moving their service offerings to the now-maturing ServiceOntario counters as had been done voluntarily by other ministries. I was met with quiet resistance by two ministries in particular, which together were in the business of issuing important identification documentation. I heard concerns from the respective deputy ministers about the security implications of transferring their ministries' counter services to others, worries about a loss of service quality and the loss of a direct chain of accountability between ServiceOntario and their minister. This was not the only time that I was forced to nudge some deputy ministers to support important changes.

I moved forward by deciding that this would no longer be a voluntary venture. ServiceOntario would have several months to work out the issues with the outlier ministries, with an emphasis on understanding their concerns about service quality, developing a plan to mitigate risks, and negotiating the transfer of resources, which had also become a tender issue. At the same time, responsibility for ServiceOntario was transferred to a senior deputy minister in a powerful central agency. This was a touchy process and required sustained leadership, which included invoking the premier's personal interest in seeing this project fully achieved (I made sure that the premier understood why this was important). These efforts were ultimately successful and the merged service organization has worked well since. The process was assisted by the consolidation of associated HR capacity, IT, and financial resources in one governing location. Equally important was a willingness to listen to the understandable concerns of the outlier ministries and to address them. My sustained interest in this file (which was on more than one occasion described as "unhealthily obsessive" by deputy ministers), was later identified by both participants and observers in the process as a key success factor. This really came down to doing the right thing.

SERVICE CANADA

Service Canada is described as a one-stop delivery network providing access to over seventy-seven different Government of Canada programs, with a strong focus on transactional services such as benefit payments. Citizens can access Service Canada in person at one of 329 Service Canada Centres or 222 outreach and mobile sites, online and through various free phone numbers. Service Canada also operates the Government of Canada's 1-800-O-CANADA national telephone line where citizens can access general information on the comprehensive range of programs and services available to Canadians (UK Cabinet Office 2009, 37).

The organization's mandate is to make access to federal government programs and services faster, easier, and more convenient. This must be pursued in the context of also maintaining a national government presence across the full geographic breadth of Canada, and its population of 35.54 million.[20] In 2009-10, Service Canada handled 9.7 million visitors at points of service; served 7.7 million clients in person; responded to 58.6 million phone calls; received 55.1 million website visits; and paid out more than CAD$88 billion in benefits. Earlier data (2007-08) showed over 90 per cent of the most commonly requested government services are available online. Eighty-four per cent of service users are happy with the overall levels of service received from Service Canada. Service Canada has also entered into some significant vertical service delivery partnerships, although many of these have been initiated by Canadian provinces. Responding to considerable effort from Ontario, Service Canada worked with ServiceOntario to co-locate federal, provincial and municipal services in a flagship office location in Ottawa. There is also an online process, long promoted by Ontario, for parents of newborns to register the birth of their child municipally, and receive a provincial birth certificate, federal Social Insurance Number and child tax benefits in one application in six provinces. The next phase involved the creation of a single automatic application process for all services relating to newborns. This is a good example of the use of digitization to seamlessly share records across jurisdictional boundaries.

This is a key juncture for federal-provincial service delivery relationships for several reasons. First, federal-provincial cooperation on service delivery is deepening, although slowly and intermittently. The federal government has established a federal/provincial/territorial council of deputy ministers as a focal point for planning, architecture and delivery. Second, the federal government has shifted from follower to partner in seeking additional arrangements with provinces and territories to extend the "bundling" of federal and provincial service offerings. Third, the fiscal imperative is growing. All of Canada's governments are facing difficult fiscal challenges that will inevitably create pressure for further reforms. Fourth, Canada's federal and subnational jurisdictions have considerable experience in transferring services through uploading or downloading arrangements. For example, there is a trend towards the federal government assuming responsibility for administering provincial corporate, sales, and income taxes. In the other direction, most provinces have assumed responsibility for employment supports and the provision of support to new immigrants. All of these arrangements are based on the benefits of scaling up and integrating transactional and professional services at a single level. In larger provinces such as British Columbia and Ontario, this has resulted in the consolidation of employment support services that were previously provided by all three levels of government.

Some consensus is emerging on shared priorities for transformation. Four priority areas have been identified by federal and provincial officials for further attention:

> *Service Bundling:* major life and business events such as births, bereavement, and business registration and regulation;

> *"Smart Footprint":* providing a broad range of access points such as front counter, telephone, and web-based, and encouraging automated self-service functions, which increase speed of delivery and minimize costs (for example, the automated renewal of a business or hunting licence with the ability to print an instant licence at home or in a local library);

> *A Service-Oriented Approach:* to achieve administrative efficiencies by moving to horizontal governance approaches that foster collaboration and innovation, while maintaining the vertical accountabilities associated with legislative responsibilities; and,

> *Enabling Tools:* for example, working through other inter-jurisdictional forums to examine the possible use of the national Business Number as a single identifier for businesses.

There is interest at all levels of government in joining up information platforms for purposes of identity authentication as well as more rapid sharing of information on life events (for example, information sharing agreements on bereavement have resulted in fewer cases of pension over-payment and will likely be a tool in combating identity theft). This form of digital integration is expected to grow. Senior federal and provincial officials see a shift away from the trend of physical common front counters and towards virtual co-location and bundled online service offerings. This moves Canada into the domain of "digital era governance" (Dunleavy et al. 2006). Also expected is a focus on collaboration on common research interests, including privacy and the use of informed consent to enable the sharing of data and a "Tell Us Once" principle across multiple program areas (allowing service users to simultaneously notify multiple government agencies of a change in address and other changes in circumstance in one transaction).

On the challenge side, the creation of a corporate back office platform that would ideally support integrated front counters and websites has been very slow in materializing. As a result the siloed nature of departments, together with the fragmentation of back office services, including IT, have posed some serious challenges in accelerating service integration at the federal level. This was highlighted in the Clerk of the Privy Council's annual report for 2010-11 (2011). This stands as a good example of the nonlinear aspects of public service reforms. This changed in August 2011, when the president of the federal Treasury Board announced the creation of Shared Services Canada, accountable for the development of corporate IT and procurement systems and other consolidated "back office" systems. Perhaps fittingly, the head of Service Canada was assigned to lead the creation of Shared Services Canada.

In 2014, as part of the federal public service's effort to renew public services, Wayne Wouters, then the Clerk of the Privy Council, launched "Destination 2020" outlining a vision for the public service. The vision's four major themes are consistent with some of the key themes discussed in this book:

- An open and networked environment that engages citizens and partners; a whole-of-government approach that enhances service delivery and value for money;

- A modern workplace that makes smart use of new technologies to improve networking, access to data, and customer service; and

- A capable, confident, and high-performing workforce that embraces new ways of working and mobilizing the diversity of talent to serve the country's evolving needs (2014).

Destination 2020's focus on networks includes building better relationships with the private and not-for-profit sectors and working more closely with other levels of governments, partners, and end users in the design and delivery of public programs. The whole-of-government element of the vision speaks to building an enterprise-wide management culture and supporting structures to enhance collaboration on complex, cross-cutting issues and solutions; and the widespread adoption of common and shared service functions such as HR, pay, and benefits to drive down costs. There is also a commitment to ongoing program review with an explicit reference to examining opportunities for alternative delivery (2014).

ASSESSING PROGRESS

Service Canada has made significant, although incremental, progress along the trajectory of service integration. As a national jurisdiction it has done well in establishing an integrated service delivery system in a huge country with a greatly dispersed population. In doing this, it has overcome the challenges of scale that seem to hinder national level programs in larger countries (Dean 2009). It has also achieved this in the absence of a fully integrated corporate IT platform and integrated HR capacity of the sort envisaged by the proposed Shared Services Canada organization.

A significant success factor in integration is effective and resilient horizontal governance, both within and between levels of government. In this respect, officials point to the importance of the intergovernmental deputy ministers' committee, and to some influential memoranda of understanding between federal/provincial/territorial Cabinet secretaries and between ministries and departments. Kernaghan (2007) confirms this in a study of barriers to further joint federal-provincial service initiatives. In 2004, Alex Himelfarb, the federal Clerk of Canada's Privy Council and I, in the role of Ontario's Secretary of Cabinet signed a memorandum of agreement between the governments of Canada and Ontario committing to accelerate joint approaches to service delivery and focus on several priorities. In an unusual, if not unprecedented, step this memorandum was circulated to the public service executive cadres of both organizations. This was more than a communications tool. It provided explicit direction and permission to staff to act and also reinforced the efforts of "change activists" in the middle and lower levels of the two organizations. The content of the memorandum was later converted into an agreement signed by ministers representing the two levels of government (Ontario Newsroom 2004). This was an unusual example of collaborative public service leadership across jurisdictional boundaries. It was also a top-down effort to encourage both horizontal and bottom-up momentum. In Ontario, support came from the critical middle management layer of the public service in the form of the activist Provincial Interministerial Councils, a group of change ready public sector entrepreneurs who effortlessly crossed ministry and jurisdictional boundaries to get things done.

But just as ServiceOntario stumbled at the mid-point of its reform journey, its federal counterparts are reported to have lost some momentum as well, moving slowly and cautiously down the road towards fully integrating services. In a review of federal progress in developing horizontal management Lindquist (2012) commented on the pace of reforms. He points to messy intergovernmental politics and the traditional challenge of turf protection by officials and ministers. He also explores a conflict within the federal biosphere between top-down versus bottom-up approaches to horizontal management; risk aversion in the context of working with a command and control government, and the absence of appropriate capacity and resources. Lindquist regards capacity building as a bridge between top-down and bottom-up approaches to horizontal management. While at one level this dichotomy might represent competing visions of implementing desired change there is, in practice, nothing incompatible about them. And neither would be optimal on its own. As discussed in the next chapter on leadership, the challenge for senior leaders is finding the right mix of top-down and bottom-up strategies based on the characteristics of an organization, the nature of the changes desired and the degree of urgency in getting the job done.

Senior federal government practitioners have identified the following challenges in extending integrated approaches to service delivery:

1. The capacity of potential service delivery partners to deliver (including their human resource capacity).

2. Insufficient federal government presence at the community level, sug-gesting a need for greater collaboration with municipal government.
3. Problems of inter-operability between different information technology systems and the upfront costs of new technology.
4. Problems with data sharing, including concerns about privacy issues.

The first two of these issues relate to the concept of senior levels of govern-ment intervening to build stronger partnerships and to grow the capacity of a "public service economy" (Sturgess 2012).

Evert Lindquist's (2012) stock-take of federal initiatives is insightful, especially in pointing to the importance of leadership and capacity build-ing. Kernaghan's advice on governance instruments is similarly valuable. This chapter also points to the importance of both top-down and bottom-up approaches to organizational change, the importance of lining up back office services such as IT with the reform of integrated front counter and web-based service delivery, and the challenges of scale in national level reforms. Added to this advice should be the importance of governments taking their lead from citizens as services are being reviewed, redesigned, and implemented. Canada is a leader in measuring citizen expectations and satisfaction with govern-ment services but what governments hear is not always reflected in programs and activities. Progress is being made but additional momentum is necessary.

PART TWO: EMERGING EFFORTS TO INTEGRATE HUMAN SERVICES IN CANADA AND THE UNITED KINGDOM

In this section we look at opportunities and practices associated with the delivery of human services. This range of services includes supports in areas such as income security, employment assistance, social and community ser-vices, housing, children's services, disability support, Aboriginal affairs, and domestic and family violence services. Unlike many generic transactional counter services, the provision of human services must be responsive to the personal needs of clients, many of whom are reliant on support from several ministries or agencies. The drivers of reform in this area are similar to those prompting integration of transactional services. However, in view of the burgeoning costs and service gaps in social and community services, child welfare, mental health, and social housing, the potential client service and efficiency dividends arising from integration are much greater. In certain circumstances, integrating human services can improve services to clients (especially those with multiple needs), resulting in more efficient use of human and fiscal resources, and better connecting investments to tangible outcomes.

As noted earlier, while Canada has been a pacesetter in the integration of transactional services delivered to citizens, there has been considerably less focus at the federal and provincial levels on joint approaches to the delivery of human services. For Canada and in particular its provinces/territories and municipalities, joined-up approaches to human services represents the next frontier in service delivery (Dean 2009). Integrated approaches will involve both vertical collaboration between levels of government, as well as new forms of networked horizontal collaboration involving municipalities, social enterprises, and not-for-profit and private sector delivery organizations.[21] Given the federal government's limited role in human service delivery, the major locus of intergovernmental collaboration in this area will involve provincial and municipal governments. Where the federal government is funding these services through its health and social transfers, however, it could tie those transfers to desired policy outcomes and to the development of more integrated approaches to delivery. At the provincial level, rapidly escalating health care costs – until recently growing at over six per cent annually, and occupying almost half of provincial spending — are prompting greater collaboration between hospitals and community care organizations.

A 2013 report based on a survey of twenty-two national and sub-national jurisdictions identified five key trends in this area:

1. A personalized approach to supporting service users through complex care journeys or "client pathways".
2. Changes to funding structures to incent desired outcomes.
3. Improved coordination between governments to address service and funding silos and build integrated case management systems.
4. Inter-sectoral integration involving new forms of horizontal partnership with the private and not-for-profit sectors.

5. Place-based integration, which reflects a growing belief that complex social problems are better addressed through coordinated local interventions (Gold and Dragicevic 2013, 5-6).

There are numerous Canadian initiatives designed to integrate the delivery of human services that are reflective of the five trends noted above. These efforts have been sporadic and isolated but momentum is growing (Gold and Hjartarson 2012). In particular, there has recently been an increased emphasis in the health care field on personalizing patient pathways through the continuum of hospital and community or home care by better connecting service providers or offering the support of "patient navigators." An effort is also being made in many parts of Canada to divert non-urgent emergency room visits by creating more integrated patient records that are available to a network of potential providers. Digitization is playing an important role in the integration agenda as paper-based patient records and diagnostic results are transferred to digital media and more easily and quickly shared (Gold and Hjartarson 2012, 19).

Three Canadian cases are discussed below, followed by a discussion of the trajectory of reform in the UK and the presentation of reforms in Scotland.

ALBERTA MINISTRY OF HUMAN SERVICES

In a direct response to the siloed architecture of government, the government of Alberta has consolidated programs responsible for Aboriginal support, children, family, social and community services, benefits, and the homeless within a new Ministry of Human Services. This was done with the explicit intention of furthering service integration and increasing partnerships with community-level providers. "Human Services' mission is to assist Albertans in creating the conditions for safe and supportive homes, communities and workplaces so they have opportunities to realize potential. Its core business is to work collaboratively with government, community, partners and stakeholders to deliver citizen-centred programs and services that improve quality of life for Albertans" (Alberta Ministry of Human Services 2014). The convergence of these programs creates the potential for greater policy coherence, better informed program design, and more integrated forms of service delivery. The focus on increased collaboration with community partners reflects a growing recognition of the social capital resident in communities as well as the realization that local service delivery tends to be more responsive to community needs.

From the outset, the new ministry was launched as a completely new organization to avoid the perception of some programs joining a core predecessor ministry, and to offset efforts to protect previously held turf. Eighteen months of engagement with stakeholders and the ministry's 7,000 staff on the shape and nature of integrated service models was considered an important foundational investment. Recognizing the scale of the organizational transformation, a Chief Strategy Officer and Chief Diversity Officer were appointed to work with the deputy minister in leading the process. An early requirement was the consolidation of the twenty-seven regional boundaries collectively established by predecessor programs down to seven. The consolidation paved the way for the development of a more streamlined budget model under which regional budgets are aggregated, giving program managers more flexibility to shift resources to emerging or changing priorities or place-based service requirements. A new integrated service delivery model focused on joining up front-line professional staff to better serve multiple needs clients. In parallel, front counter disability offices ("Alberta Supports") were asked to assume more responsibility for processing client applications, removing the administrative burden from professional staff who are now able to devote more time to helping clients. One unforeseen outgrowth of integrating fragmented programs has been that an "Employment First" program, which focuses on supporting the employability of social assistance recipients, is now being extended to recipients of Alberta's long-term disability program. Ministry leaders surmise that this would not have occurred in the absence of co-location of the two disability support programs and the development of closer links with the disability community following the creation of the new ministry.

As might be expected, the most significant challenges reported by program leaders arise from the turbulence of regional realignment, some turf protection, and necessary adjustments by some previously "large fish" in relatively small ministries who are now part of a larger enterprise and working alongside other powerful programs. The up-front investment in engaging staff and stakeholders in discussions about the shape and advantages of integration is reported to have been important in ameliorating these concerns. The consolidation of fragmented IT platforms is a work in progress with the result that, in the interim, call centre staff must still obtain data from several separate data sources.

THE REGION OF PEEL

At the municipal level, the Region of Peel in Ontario initiated a program in 2007 to integrate its fragmented human services functions into a new Human Services Department. This was prompted by budget pressures and the realization that its siloed organizational structure was not responsive to the needs of clients, especially those with complex needs who required support from more than one service area (Gold and Hjartarson 2012). Children's, social, and housing services were delivered separately across two departments, with each service area maintaining siloed client records and operating with separate budgets.

The staging of reforms appears to have benefited from reflection on practice elsewhere. The first stage of reform, in 2007, saw the new Human Services Department integrate the previously separate social services, housing, and property departments. The new department also provided a legal mandate for both full integration and the accountability to get the job done. In 2008, a two-year period of consolidating back office services was launched, starting with finance, IT and professional development. These services were integrated in a new Integrated Business Services Division. In a third stage, between 2008 and 2011, programs providing direct service delivery were integrated and a one-window point of access was created for online and telephone services. In the fourth and final stage of the project, an integrated case management system is being put in place, which will permit either single caseworkers or multi-disciplinary teams to access client files and monitor their progress. The data will also enable the department to track clients' outcomes.

The new organization has helped the Region absorb the growth in demand for human services, refocused delivery towards proactive interventions and resulted in increased client satisfaction (Gold and Hjartarson 2012, 32-37).

In the course of a discussion with senior executives in the region I asked for their wish list of actions the provincial government could take to help accelerate the process of integration. Three things were mentioned. First, provincial privacy legislation, which defines ministries or other major organizational units as separate institutions precludes the sharing of personal records across departmental boundaries. This has been a major legislative roadblock in developing integrated client records and can only be addressed by provincial intervention. Second, the province could provide greater latitude for the consolidation of funding across currently stove-piped budget lines (consolidating budgets for preventing and treating alcohol and drug abuse, for example).

It is notable that none of these requested provincial interventions involved an ask for additional financial resources.

And third, streamlining the "web of rules" associated with eligibility for social assistance support. The interpretation of these complex rules consumes a disproportionate share of caseworkers' time (Lankin and Sheikh 2012). It is notable that none of these requested provincial interventions involved an ask for additional financial resources. On the contrary, positive responses on the part of the province would result in improved services to vulnerable citizens and an efficiency dividend. There is an important lesson for governments here.

EMPLOYMENT PROGRAM OF BRITISH COLUMBIA

The Alberta and Region of Peel cases tackled organizational silos by changing the architecture of their organizations. Other jurisdictions have looked for opportunities to bundle like services behind common counters and websites in the vein of the ServiceOntario model. In the wake of federal-provincial agreements under which some federal labour market services have been devolved to provinces, several provinces have adopted this bundled approach to service provision.

In April 2012, the Employment Program of British Columbia (EPBC) was launched as a provincial one-stop employment program. EPBC replaced several federally- and provincially-funded employment programs and services, including a community assistance program, bridging programs and an employment program for persons with disabilities. The EPBC integrates these former services into a single, comprehensive employment program. EPBC services include self-serve job search services, client needs assessment, case management and other employment service options for those needing more individualized services, to prepare for, find and maintain sustainable employment (Ministry of Social Development and Social Innovation 2014).

EPBC services are delivered through WorkBC Employment Services Centres (ESC), which offer individualized, in-person help to clients. The ministry has established seventy-three contracts for delivery of EPBC services, based on eighty-five geographic catchment areas that span the province. Each area has a minimum of one service centre and offers outreach and itinerant services. Catchment areas were designated to ensure equitable access to the program, and to allow program delivery to be tailored to the needs of specific geographic regions and local community requirements.

BC has also developed an Integrated Case Management (ICM) system. This is a partnership between several provincial ministries designed to consolidate client information on one platform. Staff and service providers only have access to information that is necessary for a specific purpose, to allow them to do their jobs and deliver services. Where a client transfers between communities their case file information can be accessed by service centre staff in the new location. British Columbia's Privacy Commissioner is reported to have been heavily involved in monitoring ICM development from the outset of the initiative with the result that the sharing of client data has not been an issue from a privacy perspective.

The ICM also incorporates a financial management system and is used to process all invoices related to client support. It is also used to gather data and information to assist in measuring performance and client outcomes. Importantly, funding is partially tied to desired outcomes.

As part of EPBC, the Ministry of Social Development and Social Innovation has implemented a community and employer partnerships initiative with the goal of increasing employment opportunities for unemployed British Columbians through the use of agency and business partnerships, shared information and technology, and innovative processes and practices. Through this program, businesses, non-profit organizations, crown corporations and municipalities may apply for time-limited community-based projects that result in, or eventually lead to sustainable employment. With a short couple of years of experience under its belt the program will be the subject of a rigorous external evaluation process beginning in 2014. The evaluation will determine whether the program is meeting its intended principles, outcomes, and objectives. It will also answer specific questions, developed in consultation with stakeholders (including clients), to gain insights into: the success and impacts of the program; the design and delivery of the program; and, program sustainability. The evaluation is also expected to highlight any unintended consequences flowing from the reform.

This case is of interest for several reasons. First, it grew out of the Canadian government's program review exercise in the mid-1990s and a core business review that resulted in federal programs and funding being devolved by the federal government subject to periodic agreement on program objectives. This is an example of contracting within the public sector as well as a sensible vertical realignment and consolidation of programs. It has eliminated program duplication and provided for the pooling of previously stove-piped funding. Most importantly however, it is resulting in a stronger and more relevant suite of integrated employment services for citizens.

INTEGRATING HUMAN SERVICES IN THE UNITED KINGDOM

The sweeping changes to the economy and culture of the United Kingdom initiated by Prime Minister Margaret Thatcher in the early 1980s launched a vigorous debate about the future of public service delivery, which remains unabated. The UK has become a laboratory for a radical approach to public service reform which has been reignited by the global recession triggered in 2008 and the deep cuts in public spending that have followed. The 2012 "Comprehensive Spending Review" involved the deepest cut in public sector spending since World War II.

Standing alongside the government's expenditure constraints is Prime Minister Cameron's vision of the "Big Society", which envisages a radically decentralized Britain in which department-based programs are dramatically scaled back or set aside, with more funding being provided directly to schools, general practitioners, individuals and communities. This might be described as a strategy to tackle departmental siloes in government by going around or over them and creating a direct relationship between government funding agencies and local delivery organizations. The Big Society, which emphasizes building with social capital rather than government spending, envisages a more active role for the social sector, with volunteers, charities, and social enterprises filling the gaps left behind by a smaller government (Cabinet Office 2010).

The concept of "joined-up" government has been a key part of the nomenclature of public service reform in the UK for the past twenty years as the experimentation with public service reforms launched by Thatcher continued under the Labour administrations of Tony Blair and Gordon Brown, and subsequently under the coalition government led by David Cameron. The most significant breakthroughs in joint delivery have emerged from central government efforts to encourage cross-departmental collaboration to support the implementation of political priorities. As noted earlier, the creation and achievements of the Prime Minister's Delivery Unit and the hands-on leadership of Blair has been well documented by Sir Michael Barber in *Instruction to Deliver* (Barber 2007).

The UK's progress on integrated approaches to transactional service delivery has been moving slowly despite government-commissioned reports outlining integration opportunities (Varney 2006). Directionally, UK's government appears to be leapfrogging physical co-location of services and moving directly to virtual integration, which coincides closely with the direction now being taken by Canadian reformers (Dean and Boutilier 2012). While public service delivery in developing countries is outside the scope of this book, it is important to note that mobile phone technology and Internet-based services are fast becoming the foundational platform for the provision of information, financial services (including micro financing) and public services in those countries. This includes the management of public health, education, the provision of subsidized food and the availability of critical information on fertilizer and crop process to rural populations. Developments in Kenya, India, and Ethiopia are explored by Bhatnagar (2014). The developed countries of the northern hemisphere could learn much from the developing world's experimentation with the use of mobile phone technology as a hub for public information and public service delivery.

INTEGRATING HUMAN AND JUSTICE SERVICES – PLACE, PERSONALIZATION AND POOLED BUDGETS

In a more transformative sense there are significant efforts under way in the UK to tackle tough and complex challenges in the arena of human services, and especially in relation to individuals and families with complex needs. These are the "wicked" policy challenges public service managers often refer to as the "next frontier" in reforming service delivery (Dean 2009). This frontier includes addressing issues such as long-term unemployment, problem families, re-offenders in the justice system, and children, seniors and persons with disabilities in need of complex care.

There are a number of antecedents to this development: A shift in thinking on the part of the Blair government away from central command and control management and towards user engagement and partnerships with front-line providers (Cabinet Office 2008); the large and growing costs associated with health, community, family and justice services in the context of massive deficits; and the increasing prevalence of local and entrepreneurial efforts to join up services around special needs individuals, families and social issues. At the heart of this shift have been a number of objectives shared, across ideological boundaries, by Prime Ministers David Cameron, Tony Blair and Gordon Brown. This commonality of vision on the part of three very different prime ministers is rarely mentioned.

Taken together these objectives move beyond notions of "joined-up government". Rather, they imply boundary-less vision of disintermediated services in which budgets are pooled to better address previously intractable social issues. The focus has shifted to communities or "place" (Dunleavy 2010), and a broad range of networked service providers engaging more closely with customers and clients.

Common elements of this approach include:

- Greater personalization of services in relationships of "co-production." This personalization allows service users to engage with providers in developing service plans (for example, recent approaches to employment supports in the UK and Australia);

- A shift from cross-departmental collaboration at the national level to a whole-of-system approach. This brings together local government, front-line professionals and other providers from multiple organizations with the goal of wrapping services around the complex needs of clients. There is an increased use of "system navigators" or case managers with access to pooled budgets and the ability to commission a range of services;

- Increased devolution of service delivery and budgets to local authorities and front-line professionals. Such devolution allows government to focus more on strategy (for example, the Cameron government's Localism legislation and the National Health Service reforms that envisage general practitioners commissioning a broad range of health services at the local level); and,

- Greater involvement of social enterprises, charities, voluntary organizations, and the private sector. This cooperation results in a networked system of delivery as envisaged under the banner of the "Big Society" and outlined in the Open Public Services White Paper (Cabinet Office 2011).

TOTAL PLACE AND COMMUNITY BUDGETS

All of the above features are present in the "Total Place" initiative, which started under the Labour government in April 2009 just as the UK had entered a period of severe fiscal crisis. Total Place originated in an operational efficiency report led by Lord Michael Bichard, which promoted a whole-system approach to public service delivery. The report concluded that a step change was required in breaking through or dodging around numerous local and national government departmental silos. Bichard recommended that local pilots be established to determine the extent to which collaborative place-based strategies, designed with community involvement, and with access to pooled budgets, could better tackle complex and persistent social issues.

Thirteen pilot sites were chosen across the country with each choosing one or more cross-cutting and complex community problems such as, offender management, drug and alcohol abuse and special needs children or seniors (Leadership Centre for Local Government 2010).

In each pilot a three-phase process was put in place. First, there was a count of all money ostensibly targeted at a social challenge or opportunity. Next, the aggregated existing spend was then mapped along its course through siloed departments and agencies to identify how the money was flowing and for what purpose, and to identify duplication and redundancy. In a third phase a process was set in place to assess local relationships and capacity, degree of communications flow, interactions and partnerships.

The process also placed an emphasis on community and customer insights, looking at the degree of uptake of current services and what services people actually wanted. The subsequent reports made recommendations and proposals on more effective ways of deploying pooled budgets to focus on costly problem areas. They included plans for greater collaboration and integration of local service providers, greater community involvement and new or amended central/local governance arrangements. This was completed between June and November 2009, with the thirteen local reports being consolidated and submitted to the Treasury department for the budget process.

The devolution of this task to local leaders and organizations was matched with the involvement of senior departmental leaders ("Barrier Busters") from key national government departments at a steering table chaired by Lord Bichard. The pilots were welcomed by local leaders and are reported to have improved local level communications, collaboration and partnerships as well as building stronger and more trusting relationships between local communities and their central government counterparts. (Leadership Centre for Local Government 2010). For example, the County of Durham undertook an analysis of the impacts of the totality of funding that it receives and the way this is deployed in some of the country's more challenging areas. Durham's initial findings show that the housing-related public funding they received in 2007-08 was spread across thirteen significant funding streams and a number of smaller scale streams. They moved on to examine the specific local impact of this complex funding landscape and how it can be reshaped to maximize the use of both public and private spending in the area to better meet the needs of residents.

The pilots identified three major challenges in moving forward:

1. Performance management frameworks had grown cumbersome (requiring some areas to report to several government departments on 1,000 indicators).
2. Strict "ring fencing" of budgets (for example, separate budgets for alcohol and drug programs makes it harder to develop broader addictions strategies).

3. Putting customers at the heart of service design (for example, "wrap-around" and localized models should replace traditional one-size-fits all service design being driven from central government).

Changes introduced by both the Brown and Cameron governments have now addressed these concerns. Local performance management frameworks have been updated and standardized and 180 national indicators were slated to be reduced to no more than twenty. "Ring fencing", the allocation of funds for only one specific purpose, is being removed for upwards of 90 per cent of national funding transfers to local government.

Success factors associated with Total Place/Community Budget pilots include:

- Securing local involvement in the central government's policy development processes;

- Having pilots developed and led locally, with support, but not direction, from the UK government;

- Loosening up ring-fenced budgets in order to provide local flexibility in aligning funding with local priorities;

- The presence of pre-existing entrepreneurial leadership and/or a pre-existing culture of collaboration and working across boundaries; and,

- Building relationships based on mutual trust (DeBeer 2010).

Following the 2010 general election, Prime Minister Cameron affirmed the importance of the Total Place policy framework, re-branding it as "Community Budgets" with an announcement of support for the pre-existing pilots as well as expansion of the original number of pilots from thirteen to sixteen. Consistent with the themes of Total Place, Cameron wants a focus on families with complex needs. As noted earlier, it is estimated that there are 120,000 "troubled" families with complex needs in the UK, which collectively absorb several billion pounds in spending, with the vast majority this being spent on amelioration of damage already done as opposed to prevention.

Cameron wants to see an increased emphasis on national-local partnerships to tackle reoffending, issues associated with drugs and alcohol, and on greater flexibility for national job centres to work with local governments.[22]

INTEGRATED APPROACHES TO TACKLE COMPLEX SOCIAL ISSUES

Two UK initiatives stand out as having both a community focus and a design that sees multiple services aligned to "wrap around" complex needs clients: the North Liverpool Community Justice Centre (see Dean and Boutilier 2012) and "Getting It Right For Every Child" in Scotland, which we explore below.

Getting it Right for Every Child (GIRFEC) was launched in response to an increasing number of referrals to the Children's Reporter. It was formalized in a 2008 agreement between the Convention of Scottish Local Authorities (COSLA) and the government in Scotland, which provided for the establishment of community planning partnerships. The vision for GIRFEC is the replacement of a siloed set of health and human services with a "wrap-around" model in which professionals and organizations collaborate to develop high quality interventions for high needs clients (Government of Scotland 2014).

GIRFEC's principles are:

• Putting the child at the centre;

• Developing a common language and common assessment tools to enable services to flow around clients; and,

• Developing and emphasizing clear expectations, principles and values to encourage collaboration between professionals.

Previously, professionals worked in silos and developed separate reports on the child whereas they now work together and with the family to develop a single integrated plan for the child and family. Eight common assessment indicators are used together with a common risk/resilience matrix. A lead professional or "system navigator" is designated as the main point of contact for the family. Consolidating a large number of referral forms used by siloed agencies has resulted in a reduced administration load for front-line professionals (from 30 per cent of their time down to 10 per cent). Within the first twelve months of operation, caseloads for social workers dropped, on average, by 50 per cent, allowing a more concentrated focus on a smaller number of the toughest problem cases. Police saw the biggest jump in resource demands because they no longer automatically refer children's issues to the child protection system. Police now communicate directly with social workers, activating faster responses to incidents or indicators of potential harm to children.

Researchers at Edinburgh University evaluated GIRFEC in 2009, finding that two-thirds of families needing multi-agency support reported improvement in service. One client reported, "It felt like a team, we couldn't tell whether the person that we were talking to was a social worker or a health visitor", and they are now working with, and cared for, by a single team, rather than repeating their story to many different professionals. In addition, diverse professionals become engaged as part of the support team. In cases of domestic violence witnessed by children on weekends, for example, the children's teachers are informed by the police prior to school opening on Monday morning, providing the teacher an opportunity to support the child and call on further levels of professional support if appropriate (GIRFEC senior staff cited by Dean and Boutilier 2012, 33).

Government officials report that key levers in implementation have been the formation of community planning partnerships involving police, local councils, and social service organizations; the creation of integrated service area managers with an ability to operate across service boundaries; and, professionals empowered to work across boundaries. To support the management of information, the social work service has provided a secure computer network for client files. Managing information is said to be "tricky, because information means different things to different professionals ... for police it can be evidence, while for general practitioners such data is regarded as protected and private ... these things can't be legislated, they have to be worked out" (2012, 33). Similarly, decisions about the designation of a lead professional are made on a client-focused basis (the person who best knows and has the trust of the child and family) but this has been challenging where the composition of a case team and designation of a lead professional does not fully align with the formal authority to make referrals to other professionals.

GIRFEC is facing several other challenges. Significant changes in outcomes have not yet materialized because the program focuses on the early years through interventions that do not lend themselves to quick outcomes; budget cuts are causing partners to retract to core services; and, the large number of local authorities (32) and eight separate police forces causes difficulties in working cross-institutionally, even in the context of a relatively small country.

Scotland's government is relatively small and not as compartmentalized as the UK government, with more permeability between smaller departments. The new relationship between central and local government in Scotland is perceived to be a breakthrough, with significant momentum building on priority initiatives. Plans are now under way for a similar approach to adult social care.

CONCLUSIONS

Three overriding observations can be made on integrated approaches to service delivery:

- First, while research in this area suggests a spectrum of joint delivery approaches ranging from the integration of high-volume transactional services to the most complex human services, few countries have followed a common pathway. The UK is breaking ground in experimentation with advanced approaches to wrap-around human service provisions well before it has established fully integrated transactional services. This variability in approach offers a rich source of information and mutual learning opportunities.

- Second, as information technology investment, capacity and experimentation matures, it is becoming an increasingly critical factor in strategy development. Common to Australia, Canada and the UK is a current focus on the virtual co-location of online services and back office information sharing. Similarly, the availability of electronic client and patient records is a major factor in developing a fully informed approach to integrated case management and care.

- Third, more recent approaches to the integration of health, community and justice services are emphasizing the disintermediation of traditional service delivery chains. As in the case of Total Place/Community Budgets this includes a focus on mapping the aggregate spending of multiple siloed departments and determining how this might be allocated based on the priorities of communities. This implies a much more direct relationship between the funder and the client or local community. It suggests a transition from thinking about "joining-up" government and towards disintermediated or reshaped government and processes in which services are increasingly provided by tightly coordinated networks of local providers.

Similarly, in writing on modern regulation and the control of external harms, Malcolm Sparrow (2008) notes that, "successful efforts by regulators to address complex challenges often involve partnerships which are formed around the shape of the knots (problems) themselves, rather than recasting the problem to conform to existing institutional structures or trying to devise it along traditional or programmatic lines."

ADVICE FOR GOVERNMENTS, LEADERS AND PRACTITIONERS

- In a context in which demands for public services are increasing in parallel with fiscal constraint, government reforms must focus on delivering quality services much more efficiently. One proven means of doing this involves taking a lead from people and communities and building integrated and outcomes-based services that respond to those needs. Integration initiatives should result in overall cost reductions as duplication is eliminated, and initiatives should be subjected to rigorous assessment;

- The shift to the integration of human services is particularly important in view of the benefits for service users and burgeoning costs of these services. It should be a priority for governments considering a public service change agenda;

- Governments can provide leadership and incentives for an integration agenda but they also play a critical role in enabling transformation. My conversations with municipal public service leaders in a major region of Ontario revealed that the three major enablers they would ask of the provincial government did not have any cost implications (assistance with privacy legislation to enable client data to be shared between departments; latitude to move funding across program lines to better serve clients with multiple needs and some relaxation of the complex web of rules governing eligibility for social assistance). Similar concerns have been raised by local governments in the UK;

- Governments should be aware that sophisticated transformation efforts to build more efficient and integrated service delivery systems can be distracted or derailed by traditional across-the-board spending cuts engineered in a different part of government. As in other areas of government business, an integrated perspective should be brought to service improvement initiatives and constraint measures;

- Examining and mapping existing policy-making, service delivery and funding chains is a critical first step. There should be a tough and honest size-up of the delivery architecture across all sectors, including delivery partners and funding streams. The goal should be the development of delivery systems that provide the best experience for clients. This requires a rethink of the way governments and their processes are organized;

- The integration of back office functions must go hand in hand with the development of integrated front counters and consolidated web-based services. This brings costs down and improves internal services. While there is a significant investment involved, the development of a corporate IT platform is critical in supporting information sharing, customer relationship management and integrated client case records;

- Building high level and strategic capacity in human resources functions is also important given the role of HR in capacity development and advising on performance management, employee engagement and incentive systems;

- Integrated efforts to tackle previously intractable social issues should find a balance between upstream investments in prevention as well as in amelioration. Interventions are often weighted towards the latter;

- Given entrenched departmental and jurisdictional interests, the road to integration can be slow and difficult. In this sense, persistent high level leadership is a precondition for big breakthroughs. This is an area though where managers and leaders throughout the organization must become change activists. Many outbreaks of client-centred collaboration are occurring in the absence of strong leadership because entrepreneurial professionals are working collaboratively with partners to do the right thing for their clients. Wherever possible, this work should be documented and shared in the organization as examples of desired outcomes and ways of working. If leaders are reticent about leading, they should at the very least provide explicit permission to managers and staff to redesign delivery systems in ways that maximize service quality;

- Integration does not necessarily imply physical integration or the consolidation of departments or organizations. At a minimum it suggests collaboration and information sharing, virtual integration through electronic data sharing, online service delivery and much tighter relationships between local service providers working with common clients.

CHAPTER 8
LEADERSHIP IN THE PUBLIC SECTOR

INTRODUCTION

This chapter explores leadership in the public sector, especially in the context of reforming and improving public sector organizations, and the services they provide. It examines why public sector leadership has not shared the same profile as its private sector counterpart and considers the role of public sector leaders in both conserving public sector values while at the same time identifying and leading important change initiatives. It explores the importance of priority setting, establishing a vision for the organization, building internal and external coalitions, and driving change from the top of the organization while providing explicit permission to change ready staff and managers to innovate in their own spheres of influence. Many of the responsibilities and success factors associated with executive leadership are relevant for leaders and managers at all levels in their organizations.

The chapter concludes with a discussion of the important field of human resources management and strategy. This is a foundational element in building strong and vibrant public service organizations and yet is often marginalized, both in the literature of public administration and in public sector organizations.

I start though with some brief thoughts on my own experience as a public service leader.

LEADERS AS CHAMPIONS
OF PUBLIC SERVICES

In the context of increasingly centralized government with muscular political offices, dispersed systems of accountability, and very little political appetite for risk-taking, public servants are often challenged on how much scope they actually have to do their jobs. Paradoxically this can sometimes be viewed by political staff as a signal of reluctance to engage in difficult or contentious files. Like any other employees, public servants need to know what is expected of them, what is important to the organization, and how they are doing in delivering on expectations. They also need to know who is looking out for their interests in a context in which public services and public servants are often on the defensive in response to the theatre of politics or in face of attacks from conservative media outlets. In such cases, staff and managers look to leaders for guidance. These things will not be clear unless leaders make them explicit. In other words, public servants need champions of public services and public servants. Here are a couple of brief reflections to set the stage for what follows.

One of the biggest surprises for me in taking on a public service CEO role was the degree to which our expectations of staff and managers were assumed to be naturally understood or somehow embedded in the culture of the organization. This is often not the case. In the absence of any formal markers of what was important from the perspective of the organization, I started to develop my own sense of the organization, starting with the core services it provided: advice and support to the government of the day on policy, implementation, operations, and communications; the provision of services to citizens, and the provision of internal services within the organization. This caused me to think about the hallmarks of top-flight professional service organizations, such as listening carefully to key clients and to our own staff, measuring outcomes and thinking seriously about building the capacity of managers and staff, managing and incenting performance and recruiting and retaining the many younger professionals who are committed to public service careers. It soon became evident that managers and staff were asking similar questions. They wanted to know what they could do to make the public service successful and what success looked like in the process of serving citizens and providing the best support to the government of the day. We talked a lot about how we could optimize our capacity to deliver on these desired outcomes. This was the field in which I spent a great deal of my time as a leader. It seemed to be deeply appreciated by many staff and managers.

This is not a complex element of leadership but it is a crucial one, which requires commitment and time. It demands an understanding and recognition of the everyday reality of staff and managers, and a willingness to connect this to organizational goals and priorities, as well as translating for public servants the political frame and priorities of the government of the day.

In my early years as a deputy minister we worked for a political administration that moved into office with its policies finely tuned, with legislation drafted, and with a clear sense that it needed no policy support from the public service, which it expected to focus on implementing the government's policies. This was a legitimate political choice accompanied by crystal clear direction and, in many respects, it made the work of public servants a lot easier for a short few years. The public service became quite proficient in supporting the implementation of a large volume of manageable policy initiatives. At the same time, it was clear to me that some of that government's policy ideas were ill-conceived and would benefit from re-design or replacement by more cost-effective alternatives or ones with fewer unanticipated outcomes. As a leader I never shied away from my responsibility to offer my best professional advice, supported by evidence wherever possible, especially on potentially troubled initiatives. In my mind this was nothing more than fulfilling my professional responsibility to serve the government and the public interest.

Delivered carefully and thoughtfully, my ministry's advice was invariably received and occasionally accepted. But while acceptance was gratifying it was not the point. I considered the responsibility of public servants to be fulfilled when our best evidence, analysis and advice was provided to political decision-makers. This advice was always offered against the backdrop of our demonstrated commitment and track record in implementing political decisions to the very best of our ability. This was our job in the sometimes tricky "grey zone" in which professional public servants and political leaders and their staff intersect. There is a great deal of interest on the part of students, academic researchers, journalists, and junior public servants in this "grey" area of public service. There are several key strategies involved in navigating this terrain which should be modelled for public servants by senior public service leaders.

First, doing this reasonably well requires an understanding of the political thinking behind an initiative as well as its political objectives, which are not always aligned. So information and data that might inform an understanding of these objectives, and potential alternatives, is helpful. Second, an effort must be made to earn the trust and confidence of political actors through effective delivery of priorities and a strong service ethic. This trust is earned one transaction at a time. Third, it must be clear that this is not a point of contention or a battle about who has better evidence. It is simply about the public service fulfilling its professional responsibility to provide its best advice to the government. And once the conversation is over we have fulfilled our duty as public servants and stand ready to implement the government's decision. These approaches need to be made explicit. While we might cover them in graduate schools they must be modelled in the specific context of organizations and be adaptive to the styles of different governments. They must be modelled by leaders.

Another example of leadership practice relates to managing performance. Public service organizations, like many other organizations, are not uniformly good at managing performance. Poor performance is often tolerated for too long without honest discussions and feedback. Over time this can have a negative impact on the organization, particularly if a poor performer occupies a position of relative power and has a negative impact on the work of others. Everyone working in that context knows when this is happening so it is important to address it. I found it necessary to intervene in some of these situations, sometimes in ways that saw a senior manager departing the organization, and was surprised by the positive impact on morale and commitment in the organization. Staff and managers had seen a leader intervening in a situation that they had known for some time was counterproductive. They had seen someone make a tough decision to address a problem that had been ignored for too long. This was also a signal that poor performance was not going to be tolerated in the organization and in that sense it established an expectation that managers should be proactive in dealing with performance issues early and directly.

The lesson I took away from these experiences is that staff and managers look to their leaders for leadership and in many cases emulate it. Leaders must therefore be active in in modelling behaviour and organizational values; engaging and listening to staff; communicating expectations about the importance of sharing information and working collaboratively across ministry boundaries; building leaders behind them by giving opportunities to others; establishing and communicating priorities; in championing public services and the work of public servants; and they should be coaching and demonstrating key aspects of the public service's relationship with the political class. These are some of the things that are important about leadership in the public sector. The sections that follow discuss this further, starting with why public sector leadership is not discussed or explicitly practiced more widely.

THE SCOPE FOR LEADERSHIP IN THE PUBLIC SECTOR

Effective leadership has long been recognized as a key driver of successful organizations in the private sector and there has been a steady line of popular literature on leadership in commercial enterprises, many authored by business gurus such as John Kotter (2001), Jim Collins (2001) and Peter Drucker (2004). Each of these authors described a paradigm shift from managerial or transactional forms of leadership to the more transformative style of leadership required in a hyper-competitive, and connected, global economy. Their books have become a staple of business literature. It is a very different story for the public sector, where, despite considerable academic research and writing, there has been a striking absence of accessible literature on leadership. Jim Collins is one of the few business writers taking some time to reflect on how his own particular prescription for business success can be translated to the public sector. In *Good to Great and the Social Sectors* (Collins 2005), a monograph to accompany his bestselling *Good to Great*, Collins offers a short and very powerful explanation of why leadership matters in the public sector and how it can be exercised in a diffuse power structure. Michael Barber (2007) has written persuasively about his experience in leading the implementation of political priorities in the UK. From a practice perspective, Michael Fullan (2006) has written extensively on the role of "turnaround leadership" in improving performance in the often change-resistant education sector. Similarly, Michael Fenn (2006) has explored the complexity of leadership in the process of transformational change in his exploration of reducing wait times for critical surgical and diagnostic procedures.

Traditional conceptions of leadership assume that power and autonomy are exercised **"Even the basic** hierarchically with clear lines of influence and **vocabulary of leadership** control. But it has long been recognized that **is missing in public** leaders in large and complex organizations, **sector parlance."** especially those in the public sector, rarely expe- **—Patrice Dutil** rience such clarity. Public sector leaders start with a clearly defined accountability to elected political leaders. They operate in an intricate and complex environment with diffuse structures of power (Bourgon 2011), and they must increasingly work across organizational and jurisdictional boundaries as they navigate a more "plural" state (Osborne 2010).

In this context, Kanter (1994) has written on the value of alliances in the creation of collaborative advantage; Chrislip and Larson (1994) have explored collaborative approaches to leadership; Brown and Waterhouse (2013) have written on leading change in increasingly networked public sector systems; and Kernaghan (2003) has described the centrality of leaders as models of values-based behaviour.

Understandably, a key question for research has been the degree to which leaders have an ability to proactively intervene and influence change in public sector organizations – and if they can, should they? (Denis, Langley and Rouleau 2005, 450; Dutil 2008, 4)

This discussion has often contrasted transformative leadership (Bass 1998) and entrepreneurial approaches to leadership (Borins 2002), with a more conservative stewardship role in which public servants are positioned as stewards of public sector institutions, services and values, implementing polices and reforms decided by their political masters (Denis, Langley and Rouleau 2005, 451). Dichotomies are helpful in establishing typologies but they are seldom watertight, especially in a complex and rapidly changing environment. The lived requirements of leadership practice will in many cases result in a mix of these styles.

In *Searching for Leadership: Secretaries to Cabinet in Canada*, Dutil (2008) and others examine leadership in Westminster models of government through the lens of Cabinet Secretaries. *Searching For Leadership*, of course, implies its absence and Dutil is uncompromising about this, noting that "even the basic vocabulary of leadership is missing in public sector parlance. Distinct concepts of 'executives', 'management', entrepreneurship and leadership are jumbled together, leaving concrete examples wanting." Dutil's book shines some valuable light on this oddly-named position at the top of Westminster-style bureaucracies. Dutil says the book "advances the hypothesis that secretaries to cabinet have effectively moved beyond 'mere management' to a position where they exercise 'leadership' and explores the transition with reference to theory and practice." (2008, 14-15). He notes that studies describing the role of cabinet secretaries, and descriptions written by cabinet secretaries themselves rarely reference leadership, emphasizing instead the roles of problem solver, mediator, translator and fixer (2008, 13).

RARELY SEEN AND NEVER HEARD

In 2011, Canada's federal public service had a workforce of 282,000 (Treasury Board of Canada Secretariat 2012). In 2012, the UK's civil service had a workforce of 440,000, (the smallest since the Second World War as a result of government austerity programs). These are likely the largest employers in their respective countries but it's a good bet that the top leaders of these organizations are largely unknown, certainly outside their organizations and to a large degree inside them as well. The same is true of public service organizations around the world. It's not clear who is in charge – on the face of it, there is no chief executive officer. And yet public services are at the heart of our system of democracy. The advice and support provided to our elected representatives, the development of policies and programs and the design and delivery of crucial public services lies within the authority of public service leaders, as does oversight of spending. For example, the deputy ministers of provincial ministries of health in Canadian provinces are responsible for the disbursement of almost half of the provincial budgets. They operate in a hugely complex and demanding environment in which expectations are high and authority is broadly diffused.

Indeed, if any group of non-executive public servants are brought together, especially those working outside of provincial or national capital cities, and asked "who is in charge of the public service" it is not uncommon to hear staff say that that the national prime minister or provincial premier runs the public service. This is ultimately true in governance terms, much as it is in the case of the chair of the board of a corporation. Boards of directors are charged with setting and approving long-term policies and business strategies. They hire chief executive officers (CEOs) to run corporations and implement business strategies. And they hold their CEOs accountable for results. Likewise, prime ministers, premiers and ministers don't run public service organizations and the large majority of political leaders don't want to, although they might have some strong views on public service hiring from time to time.

There are obvious reasons for the relative invisibility of leadership in public sector organizations. The most powerful one has been touched on already. In democracies, we elect representatives to govern in the common good so accountability for the operations of governments, delivering political promises and the quality of everyday public services ultimately rests with the political leader of the governing party.

Secondly, and in parallel, the role, size and influence of the public service has evolved over time as evidenced in the position of the Cabinet Secretary or Clerk of the Privy Council. As Bourgault points out, Canada's most senior public servant, the Clerk of the Privy Council, "holds no less than four titles – clerk, secretary to cabinet, deputy minister to the prime minister and … the official 'responsible' for the administrative functioning of the Privy Council Office" (2008, 42). These titles evolved over time as an interesting reflection of the growth and increasing complexity of government operations. The first Clerk of the Privy Council in Canada (the keeper of the records) was appointed in 1867. The responsibility of Secretary to the Cabinet (translator of decisions to ministries and the public service) was added in 1940. In 1992, Canada's *Public Service Employment Act* was amended to add the title "Head of the Public Service" with responsibility for setting strategic directions for the Public Service of Canada (Bourgault 2008). In Canada, the Cabinet Secretaries in the provinces of Alberta and Ontario also hold the title of Head of the Public Service.

Despite the change in job titles, the role of elected officials and Parliament has been guarded as sacrosanct over time by those office holders, often at the expense of politicians taking on responsibility for administrative problems for which public servants should arguably be accountable. There are some exceptions to this in which fingers have been pointed in both directions. A case in point is the controversy in Canada over the "Sponsorship Program", which ran from 1996-2004 and was designed to raise the profile of the national government in the province of Québec. This has been summarized in a paper by Canadian Senator Donald Oliver: "Through the course of an audit, the Auditor General found that payments were made to advertising firms for work of little or no value. The subsequent Gomery Commission inquiry discovered that these firms then made kickbacks to officials in the then governing Liberal party. Several individuals have since been convicted of criminal offences. Ministers insisted that they had no responsibility for administration and thus were not accountable, and in turn senior public servants said they were merely implementing the wishes of ministers. In this instance, it was very difficult to identify who was accountable for ensuring that public funds were spent appropriately and thereby preventing the abuses that took place" (Oliver 2008).

While mostly hidden from view, the accountability relationship between senior public servants and their political masters has surfaced periodically in Canada in discussions about the adoption of the UK's "Accounting Officer" concept, under which senior public servants are held accountable for ministry or departmental finances. The accounting officer has been in place in the UK since 1918 but has been resisted in Canada until quite recently on the basis that it could compromise the doctrine of ministerial accountability.

The *Federal Accountability Act,* passed in 2006, instituted the position of accounting officer in Canada. Under the Act, the accounting officer is a department or agency's deputy head (the senior public servant). Within the framework of ministerial responsibility and accountability to Parliament, the accounting officer is accountable before the appropriate committees of the Senate and the House of Commons for steps taken to: deliver programs in compliance with policies and procedures; to maintain effective systems of internal control; and, to sign the accounts prepared as part of the Public Accounts, as well as for other specific duties assigned to him or her by legislation. In practice, this means the accounting officer is obligated to appear before the appropriate committees of the Senate and the House of Commons to answer questions with respect to carrying out these responsibilities.

Despite the importance of this change, the discussion of accountability officers was narrow and constrained, and tended if anything to obfuscate and bureaucratize what might otherwise have been a useful discussion about public sector leadership. Dutil (2008, 14) notes that, paradoxically, "The Gomery commission ... recommended in its final report that the role of the secretary to cabinet be redefined by eliminating its 'head of the public service' and 'deputy minister to the prime minister' designations, a move that would effectively undercut the post's leadership potential." Elsewhere, the role of head of the civil service in the UK has recently been separated from that of Secretary to the Cabinet and is now been performed as part of the responsibility of a line permanent secretary, a move that has been hotly contested in public administration circles. The report of the House of Commons Public Administration Select Committee's (2012) review of this change offers a fascinating look at the contemporary debate about public sector leadership in the UK.

In Canada, two studies have examined the role of the clerk of the privy council, one commissioned by the Gomery inquiry and the other written by Donald Savoie (1999) in his landmark book on the centralization of power in political offices in Canada. Neither study makes a single mention of leadership in relation to the role of the most senior public servant in Canada (Dutil 2008, 14). This is not a universal phenomenon in Westminster models of government. New Zealand, which has been at the radical end of public service reform for two decades and saw heavy hitting private and public sector senior managers imported into Chief Executive jobs (deputy minister equivalents) on employment contracts. The Honourable Bill English, Minister of Finance and Deputy Prime Minister had this to say about accountability: "As an incoming government in late 2008, we had a choice of ripping out 'savings' from the budget and embarking on a large-scale restructuring plan. We are not, however, doing that. We have left existing structures largely in place while establishing very clear fiscal constraints over the next four years. To do this, we are pushing the responsibility for managing resources on to our public-sector chief executives; it is not up to the Treasury or the Minister of Finance to ensure that we live within those constraints; it is up to the leadership of the separate sectors of government. We are consciously stress testing our existing, fairly devolved model of public-sector management" (English 2011). The large majority of jurisdictions, including government in Canada, are a long way from the New Zealand model but there is plenty of sensible ground in between.

LEADERSHIP WITHIN LIMITS

Public service organizations are among the largest employers in any jurisdiction and have a huge impact on the quality of government decision-making and the lives of citizens. Senior public servants exercise enormous power even within the tightly confined parameters of the governance structure within which they operate. Dutil notes:

> Cabinet secretaries "wield the influence and the authority necessary to affect how the bureaucracy chooses its priorities, builds its capacity, organizes itself for emergencies and longer-term issues, responds to political directives and accounts for its progress in meeting them ... At the same time, secretaries know that they evolve in a particularly limiting situation: they are the first servants of the state. Indeed, their role incarnates the conventional understanding that has been struck between the political and administrative spheres of governments in Canada: that the bureaucracy's mandate is to advise cabinet but, above all, execute its will. It is the secretary of cabinet's job to absorb the cabinet's wishes and determine how that body's hunches, impressions and outright directives will be acted upon" (2008, 15).

In view of these inherent tensions in the role of senior public service leaders Dutil asks a threshold question about whether cabinet secretaries exercise more than transactional functions and actually lead in transforming their organizations. The question is especially pertinent in the context of political administrations that lean towards command and control management styles, or risk-averse minority governments. The obvious answer is that cabinet secretaries *should* be leading transformation. But whether they are likely depends on the cabinet secretary and the nature of his or her relationship with their premier or prime minister. Some of the activist characteristics of public service leadership are worth exploring further.

WHAT DO WE NEED IN PUBLIC SECTOR LEADERS?

Ideal leadership attributes and priorities for public sector executives have not been widely discussed. This question is generally subordinated within discussions of managing change in the public sector (Page et al. 2012) or the challenges associated with implementing government policies (Pressman and Wildavsky 1973). Leadership is a large and complex area, which includes consideration of personal attributes, leadership styles, the manager-leader continuum and a discussion of transactional versus transformational leadership (Collins 2005).

Good public administration and citizen-centric service delivery makes for good politics.

Dutil argues that key skills include: an understanding of major issues, creating vision and setting priorities, managing competency, building networks and engaging in the search of leadership in the organization (2008, 18-32). Based on a review of practices in agencies of the government of the United States, Ingraham and Taylor identify the following five core competencies for leaders:

- leading change

- leading people

- a drive for results

- business acumen

- building coalitions and communicating (Ingraham and Taylor 2003).

In turn, Bourgault points to six types of leadership opportunities:

- counsel to political officials

- implementing the vision in the DM (deputy minister) community

- directing 'corporate governance' (providing vision and diffusing values)

- protecting conventions

- making difficult decisions, providing commitment and rallying the troops

- guiding the public service in transformation (Bourgault 2008, 67-73).

The focus in the balance of this chapter is on the importance of strong and visible leadership in the public sector and on the practices and attributes necessary for that to be successful. The starting point is the role of senior public servants in building and maintaining vibrant and successful public service organizations because, if they are not doing that, no one else will. In most cases more active public service leadership will directly benefit the political administration. One part of the leadership task involves finding the right balance between supporting the government with top-flight counsel and sound advice on policy and implementation, and leading the public service in making changes in carefully chosen areas. This must be done while serving the considerable needs of the political administration. This is not easily achieved given the demands of the political side of the ledger of responsibilities and it is far too easy to put off the leadership side of the job for another day and fill the gap with an all-staff e-mail. But leadership involves more than a communications plan. It involves conscious planning and action over a long period of time to effect change in organizations. In taking on the job of Cabinet Secretary and head of a large public service organization I made a decision to devote half of my time to leadership of the organization which, in retrospect, was barely enough.

Much is made in the literature of public administration about the line between professional or "career" public servants and elected politicians and their political staff. But the literature is silent on the point that good public administration and citizen-centric service delivery makes for good politics. Effective public services deliver a political dividend as well as a democratic dividend. Research conducted by the Institute for Citizen-Centred Service (2005) demonstrates that public services that are responsive to the needs of citizens increases confidence in government and the public sector.

Political leaders assume that public servants are striving to provide and improve public services. In the run-up to the 1995 general election in Ontario, the Mike Harris Conservatives campaigned with a promise to make government smaller. As the new premier, Harris was good to his word, eliminating 20,000 public service jobs (equivalent to 25 per cent of the workforce). But unlike other well-defined campaign commitments such as repealing the previous government's labour law and employment equity reforms, not much thinking had gone into how the public service would be reshaped in the wake of the dramatic reduction in staff.

Harris left the redesign of government services to his cabinet secretary, Rita Burak, who might have been tempted to spread the pain across the board by seeing every program shrink by 25 per cent. Burak took a more strategic perspective. She saw this as an opportunity to tackle longstanding duplication of functions across ministries and started the process of consolidating back office services, such as payroll administration, which were replicated across every ministry and agency. Burak also started the process of consolidating ministry-based service counters into the single-window ServiceOntario, which has since been emulated in many other jurisdictions. These changes saved money and improved services. They added public value.

Burak saw this as her responsibility and Mike Harris did too. None of it was easy, and it would not have happened without being driven hard from the top and with support from change ready staff and managers in the Ontario Public Service. Burak would not have flown solo on this. She would have briefed Harris regularly on progress and checked in on changes that could have a political impact (such as consolidating offices serving remote or rural communities, which were part of the Conservatives' political heartland). Harris supported his Cabinet Secretary. He respected public servants who could get the job done so he stayed out of Burak's way and focused on his political priorities. This challenges the image of Harris as a leader who had little time for the public service. Good leaders understand the need to get the right people in key jobs and to stand behind them.

Prime ministers and premiers seldom look for credit for improving public services. Public service delivery in Ontario – as it is in Canada – is mostly seen as the business of public service leaders. This is partly explained by the absence of a public and media discourse about public administration and public services. Just as in any other jurisdiction the Canadian media will report on the failure of government or the public service in the event of a tragedy in which lives are lost. But, with the possible exception of health care, there is very little interest in public administration. This contrasts to the UK where public policy and public services are staples of political and media discourse. This is reflected in the UK's parliament in the lively and informative discussions of the Parliamentary Select Committee on Public Administration, and in the media by rich coverage in newspapers such as the Guardian.

What does success look like in public sector organizations? The proposition here is that it should be measured by the degree to which an organization is achieving a high performance standard in meeting the needs of internal and external clients and partners, including the government of the day, in delivering internal professional and transactional services provided within the organization, and to external recipients of government services. This includes the development of the highest possible capacity for policy-making and the effective implementation of policy, which in turn requires top-flight human resources talent.

PRESERVING INSTITUTIONAL MEMORY AND PROMOTING PUBLIC SERVICE VALUES

A professional and non-partisan public service is an important element in democratic systems of government in which governments periodically change through the electoral process. A public service without political allegiances is considered crucial for the continuity of good governance and effective public services. This is never more important than in the transition between governments when there might be some concern within a new administration about the allegiance of public servants. In working with new administrations, public servants at all levels, and especially those working closely with prime ministers and premiers, are held to their highest professional test and must literally earn the

> "Leaders must serve not only as exemplary models of values-based behaviour, but also as skilful practitioners of the art of values management."
> — Kenneth Kernaghan

trust of a new administration in every transaction, from the quality of a policy document to the availability of office supplies in their new quarters.

A second critical role of the public service is the preservation of institutional "memory" and capacity, including policy expertise, research and specialist knowledge, governance and decision-making processes and knowledge of government stakeholders and engagement processes. This reminds us again of the important role of human resource leaders and practitioners in supporting organizational renewal.

A third role involves protecting the continuity of the core mandates and values of the public service, especially in the context of new and quickly shifting organizational forms (Aucoin 1995, 46). Kernaghan (2003) emphasizes the centrality of values in public sector organizations, arguing that academics and practitioners should give more attention to embedding these values in the structures and processes of public sector organizations. He says that, "Leaders must serve not only as exemplary models of values-based behaviour, but also as skilful practitioners of the art of values management" (2003, 718). Kernaghan outlines four classes of values: democratic, ethical, professional and people values (2003, 712). It is common to see these values reflected in published codes of ethics and values for public servants and ministers, which also tend to set out the division of responsibilities between these actors.

A 1996 report by a Canadian federal deputy ministers' task force notes that public service reform "must be animated from within by sound public service values ... consciously held and daily enacted, values deeply rooted in our own system of government, values that help to create confidence in the public service about its own purpose and character, values that help us to regain our sense of public service as a high calling" (Deputy Ministers' Task Force on Public Service Values and Ethics 1996, 64). The Government of Canada's *Values and Ethics Code for the Public Sector* takes this form, leading off with a statement that, "A professional and non-partisan federal public sector is integral to our democracy." The Code also covers expected behaviours of federal public servants and the roles and responsibilities of chief executives:

> Chief executives of public sector organizations have specific
> responsibilities under the PSDPA, including establishing a
> code of conduct for their organization and an overall respon-
> sibility for fostering a positive culture of values and ethics in

their organization. They ensure that employees are aware of their obligations under this Code and their specific organizational code of conduct. They also ensure that employees can obtain appropriate advice within their organization on ethical issues, including possible conflicts of interest ... Chief executives ensure that this Code, their organizational code of conduct, and their internal disclosure procedures are implemented effectively in their organization, and that they are regularly monitored and evaluated. Chief executives of Crown corporations may rely on their boards of directors for support in this duty ... Chief executives are responsible for ensuring the non-partisan provision of programs and services by their organizations. Chief executives are subject to this Code and to the Conflict of Interest Act. (Treasury Board of Canada Secretariat 2011, Appendix).

Kernaghan (2006) reminds us that these are weighty responsibilities and must amount to more than ensuring that the code is e-mailed to staff and framed for the boardroom and lunchroom walls. All of these behaviours and values must be frequently communicated and modelled by public service leaders. In order to make a difference and become embedded in the culture of the organization they must be lived and demonstrated by leaders as an integral means of conducting business. This is especially the case when a leader is advising the government on an alternative course of action to the one preferred by political leaders. This is an example of "speaking truth to power" or, simply put, giving honest and objective advice to ministers, which is an essential part of the administrative-political relationship or "bargain". This is a broadly accepted notion and is often explored in seminars on public administration and by public servants themselves. But such advice is sometimes delivered to a political leader who is already dug-in – minds have been made up, a decision made without public service input and a news release is being prepared. I describe this to graduate students as analogous to jumping in front of a moving train. Regardless of the circumstances and potential hostility of the environment, public service policy advisors, managers and executives are duty bound to ensure that the government has considered all of the implications of a decision, even where it is constitutional and lawful. To say the least, this requires a high level of judgement and experience as well as the ability to step into the shoes and mind of a minister or prime minister in order to frame advice, and propose alternative means of achieving the desired outcomes, in a way that makes sense to the listener. In other words, it requires an ability to understand and seamlessly navigate both the political and bureaucratic worlds. I have stepped into this role with senior politicians of every political stripe. It has not always been pleasant and my advice was not always followed, but in almost every case it was appreciated, if only at a later date. Ultimately though, in situations in which a public service leader has significant concerns about the legality or constitutionality of a political proposal, or other major concerns about the public interest, this might well be a resignation issue and it probably does not hurt that public servants and political staff alike are made aware of this.

> "The Clerk is the champion of public-sector values and is personally responsible for their promotion. Through his values, commitment, discourse, decisions, presence, and leadership, he must inspire new generations of officers and managers."
> —Jacques Bourgault

Returning to an earlier point about leadership in the public service, where does accountability lie for the strength and resilience of the organization's institutional memory? Who is leading and modelling public services values and ethics, and who is demonstrating and modelling at the highest levels of the organization the practice of speaking truth to power? This is not the job of political leaders, it is up to those who serve the government of the day, and these are hugely important responsibilities. First and foremost it is the responsibility of leaders – starting with cabinet secretaries and heads of the public services, who must model these behaviours for their deputy ministers and other senior executives as well as speaking about them in every interaction with staff. As Bourgault says, "The Clerk is the champion of public-sector values and is personally responsible for their promotion. Through his values, commitment, discourse, decisions, presence, and leadership, he must inspire new generations of officers and managers" (Bourgault 2008, 74).

Many managers and leaders do not fully appreciate the impact they have on their organizations and the extent to which they can affect their organization's climate and culture and the behaviour of staff. They are significant role models and are being watched all the time for signs of what is acceptable and important. It is crucial that leaders are conscious of this because it is a powerful responsibility and force for positive change. There is an important connector here to the importance of a people strategy in government – a thoughtful and comprehensive approach to human resources leadership that will arise repeatedly below.

THE BALANCE BETWEEN PRESERVATION AND CHANGE

The professional and non-partisan role of public servants and the core values of their organizations tend not to change over time. They are part of the shared culture of organizations and are designed to guide behaviour. Leaders have a major role to play in preserving critical aspects of an organization's culture and the values that contribute to that.

Conservation is a key role of leaders but so is the calibration of the mix between continuity and change. The promotion of core values alongside identifying and leading on areas of necessary change go to the heart of a leader's job. Terry (1998) has pointed out that while public servants perform an important role in providing for continuity this can, in some cases, extend to resistance to change and inhibit an organization's ability to evolve in response to emerging challenges and opportunities. Likewise, Collins notes that, "Enduring great institutions practice the principle of Preserve the Core and Stimulate Progress, separating core values and fundamental purpose (which should never change) from mere operating practices, cultural norms and business strategies (which endlessly adapt) to a changing world" (2005, 26).

> The promotion of core values alongside identifying and leading on areas of necessary change go to the heart of a leader's job.

One of the toughest decisions for any leader lies in determining the need for change or adjustment in the organization, how aggressive the change effort needs to be, and what will be done to accomplish those changes. Very few senior managers or leaders inherit perfectly tuned, high impact organizations.

At their very best, public sector organizations are uneven in the distribution of professional talent, expertise, commitment, culture and results. Any degree of change is disruptive and will be met with some resistance and this is often enough to make many managers and leaders think twice. Public service organizations are busy enough responding to the needs of the government and external clients without another bright idea from the boss. Resistance to change also understandably flows from the past experience of long-term public servants with previously failed reform exercises, of which there are many. Given the complexities of governance, politics and culture confronting public sector leaders an obvious precondition for moving forward is a deep understanding of challenges that might be addressed and opportunities that can be pursued.

COLLINS' "BRUTAL SIZE-UP"

The first critical step for any newly-appointed leader is an appraisal of the business or mandate of the organization and its capacity to deliver on that in the most effective and efficient way. This holds true for the head of the public service as it does also for agency heads and managers of departments and work units. The question of mandate goes to what is expected of the organization by the government, its clients and its partners, including what success looks like to them and how it can be measured and reported. These questions have traditionally not been clearly answered in the public sector where, for a long time, an emphasis was placed on inputs such as money spent and inspections conducted without substantial reference to results obtained. This is changing slowly, for example in the areas of elementary and high school achievement (Barber 2007) and where an emphasis is being placed on reducing health wait times for key diagnostics and procedures (Fenn 2006). But it remains the case that there is a vast shortage of data about the impact of spending in high cost areas of public services such as the justice, health and social care sectors.

Collins (2005) points out that a rigorous evaluation of an organization requires that leaders "confront the brutal facts" – the hard realities both inside the organization and the challenges, threats and opportunities outside of it. This includes the tough and seemingly intractable challenges associated with shrinking resources and increased expectations, the political environment and workplace morale. There are challenges in every organization and many are longstanding ones left under the rug to be dealt with on another day – and for such a long time in many cases, that most of the people working in the organization know they are there and how tough it would be tackle them. Many would assume that only a major event or crisis would draw enough attention to provoke necessary changes unless a tough-minded leader comes along and declares them to be intolerable and in need of repair.

CHOOSING PRIORITIES, ESTABLISHING A VISION AND HAVING A PLAN

Leaders must decide which challenges and opportunities they want to address, bring them to the surface and tackle them. In the regulatory context, Malcolm Sparrow (2000) simplifies this by advocating that leaders identify big problems and fix them. In the context of delivering on political priorities the essence of Barber's thesis is that prioritization is a key success factor for successful delivery. For Collins, Drucker and Kotter (as well as for many managers and leaders) decisions about priorities lie at the heart of leadership. Like Sparrow, Drucker, defines leadership as the task of setting priorities and sticking to them.

The ability to read the environment, make tough choices about priorities and to create and drive a vision for the organization is at the core of leadership.

The next logical choice involves a determination about the degree and pace of change required to move forward, whether it is incremental or transformational in nature. All of this involves sound judgement in setting priorities. And it all contributes to the development of a vision for the organization. This could involve pulling an organization out of a crisis, charting a course of continuous improvement or launching the sort of transformational changes that allow cash-strapped governments to maintain and improve public services. In other cases it might involve, in the language of Collins, an effort to move organizations from good to great.

The ability to read the environment, make tough choices about priorities and to create and drive a vision for the organization is at the core of leadership. This explains why leadership is increasingly discussed in terms of driving change in organizations as opposed to preserving the status quo (see for example Eggers and O'Leary 2009; Bourgault 2008). This is also reflected in discussions of the key competencies of leaders, which generally include the ability to lead change and people, drive towards results and build coalitions (Ingraham and Taylor 2003). Eggers and O'Leary note that, "More than anything else, success requires a leader who can navigate in both the bureaucratic and political worlds, who understands the unique terrain of government on both sides" (2009, 148).

From the perspective of both political and public service leadership, the timing of electoral cycles is obviously a major factor. Continuous improvement in policy development, service delivery and the management of public finances should be woven into planning cycles, but large-scale change initiatives requiring time for solid implementation are best launched well before the midway point in electoral cycles. Particularly where there is a change in a political administration following an election, a meeting of minds between political and public service leaders is an important precondition for achieving significant public service reforms.

If it is not obvious already, leadership, except in the rarest of cases, is not an unconscious attribute that is naturally endowed upon a fortunate minority. It is a conscious activity requiring environmental analysis, an honest appraisal of challenges and opportunities, and organizational strengths and weaknesses. It also requires a plan and the determination to see it implemented. Also fundamental is the requirement to rally the organization around a leadership vision (Bourgault 2008).

IMPLEMENTATION

Figuring out a vision for the organization, together with the priorities necessary to get there are a critical first step. Implementation is a different matter altogether. The road is littered with failed efforts to change or transform organizations and every failure leaves some cynicism in its wake at all levels. The beliefs of change-resistors are confirmed and the hopes of the change-ready are shattered. At least part of the culture of change resistance in any organization lies in past experience with derailed initiatives. In many cases public sector organizations are also change-weary.

An important first step in implementing a vision and priorities is communicating them as broadly as possible and this starts with senior staff or the management team. In the case of heads of public service or cabinet secretaries it will be the deputy ministers. This is the first and most important step because without the support of this group, implementation will be an uphill slog. Support from a leader's closest cadre of senior managers or staff cannot be taken for granted and, especially in a context of collaborative leadership, must be earned (Chrislip and Larson 1994). Even where a leader is liked and respected, his or her senior team will be wondering if a new initiative has legs or if it will be quickly derailed or, worse, die a slow and painful death. As Tony Blair learned after his first several months as prime minister in the UK, even a prime minister can't write a directive to staff and assume that it will be implemented. If it is a big breakthrough initiative it must be consciously and actively led from the top. A leader's time and concentrated effort is required; only when this is demonstrated over a period of weeks and months will full commitment be realized.

If it is a big breakthrough initiative it must be consciously and actively led from the top.

The next critical audience, at least for executive leaders, is the cadre of middle managers. Mid-level managers comprise the critical mass of management expertise in the organization. They are key points of contact and information for large numbers of staff and will often be on the front-line in implementing change initiatives. Rita Burak understood this when she was driving towards consolidated service counters in Ontario ministries. She called on Provincial Interministerial Councils (PICs) comprised of middle managers who were already organizing and communicating across ministry boundaries. PICs were created in part to break down organizational silos and to develop more collaborative working relationships at regional levels. Managers involved in this effort were supportive of Burak's vision and adopted it as a priority for their councils. This turned out to be a significant factor in getting the initiative off the ground.

As one of Burak's successors, I urged the PICs to collaborate with their federal council counterparts in developing shared federal-provincial service counters, some of which also included a municipal government presence. This is an example of unleashing self-organizing activists in the middle of organizations to support a change initiative. The managers' councils were already organizing voluntarily to break down silos and were pleased to be at the centre of a corporate change initiative. The councils also provided a quick and direct way to get leadership messages out to staff, which in large organizations can sometimes be a challenge. Middle managers were also asked to provide rapid feedback on implementation challenges and their advice on how these could be addressed, which informed adjustments and design modifications. This is a key ingredient in innovation, as well as in motivation.

Setting clear expectations, drawing a picture of what success looks like, assessing performance and providing timely feedback to staff is at the heart of good management.

Direct communications with staff are obviously important too. As noted earlier, there is often uncertainty in large public sector organizations about who is actually in charge of the public service, particularly with distance from corporate head offices and urban centres. Seeing and hearing directly from senior leaders about the state of play in the organization, and receiving status reports on organizational priorities is important for staff. In outlining key opportunities for leaders, Bourgault talks about providing commitment, "rallying the troops", broadcasting a sense of mission and valuing employees (2008, 70-72). Staff must know what is important in the organization, what success looks like and the roles they are expected to play in achieving that. In this sense it is also important that they be reminded of the values and ethics of the organization – and what is being sustained, as well as about plans for change. Authenticity and honesty in talking about what works well in the organization and what must change goes a long way in the process of earning the trust and commitment of managers and staff.

In mid-career, I somewhat reluctantly sat through a three-week leadership course for private sector managers at one of Canada's top universities. One of the most basic, but important, take-aways from the course was the simple message that every employee in any organization needs to know two things: why they are there, and how they are doing. Setting clear expectations, drawing a picture of what success looks like, assessing performance and providing timely feedback to staff is at the heart of good management.

Face-to-face meetings provide an opportunity for leaders to say "thank you" for the hard work and commitment of their public service colleagues. Nothing sparks passion and commitment in public servants more than talking about the importance of the work they do and the impact that they have on people's lives each and every day. The impact public servants have on the health, safety and quality of people's lives every day is undeniable. But it goes unheralded. We don't talk about this enough. Public servants hold a huge responsibility in their hands – whether it is for the quality of drinking water, safe and successful schools, and health care that is there when we need it. Public service leaders must remind their managers and staff that their friends, relatives and neighbours rest easy at night because they are not worrying about whether their water is potable or their local hospital and school will be open the next day. They don't think about this too much, but at the root of that comfort is that the government – or in reality public servants – are taking care of these things for them. This is a powerful message.

At another level though, we often remember the leaders that have had the most impact on us not by their policy achievements, or an inspirational talk but often by small acts of professionalism, integrity or thoughtfulness. A brief word of thanks to someone at the end of a challenging day or empathy for a policy advisor who poured their heart into a long and complex cabinet proposal only to see it summarily dismissed because of a political change of direction, will be remembered for years and shared with colleagues. This speaks to the powerful impact of the small stuff. Leaders who don't get this can still be good leaders but they are missing a significant opportunity. Inspirational leadership can be demonstrated over time in small ways with individuals and small numbers of colleagues and still have a powerful impact.

BUILDING NETWORKS AND COALITIONS

Recent literature on leadership points to the importance of developing relationships with staff, stakeholders and partners as part of a broader effort to build networks of influence. It is argued that these more fluid partnerships are much more responsive to addressing challenges that transcend organizational and jurisdictional boundaries (Brown and Waterhouse 2013; Bourgon 2011; Goldsmith and Eggers 2004).

Coalition building is an important leadership strategy at every level, from relatively small but complex or controversial initiatives through to major political priorities.

Obtaining support from managers and staff for an organizational vision and key directions is a foundational task for leaders, especially where change is contemplated. Big change initiatives, whether they involve policy, service delivery or organizational change, are much more likely to be successful when they are supported by coalitions of leaders and supporters. Coalition building is an important leadership strategy at every level, from relatively small but complex or controversial initiatives through to major political priorities. In Ontario, the Provincial Interministerial Councils were an important part of Rita Burak's network of support in building a more integrated approach to delivering public services.

Stephen Goldsmith and William Eggers have written about an emerging culture of "Governing by Network" citing the example of National Park Service Superintendent Brian O'Neill. O'Neill is credited with transforming the US government's approach to managing the Golden Gate National Recreation Area from an under-funded government-run park to a "network of interlocked public-private partnerships." O'Neill said his job was to "figure out who our strategic partners should be and how to bring them together and inspire them to be a part of it." (Goldsmith and Eggers 2004, 4-5).

Jim Collins talks about Frances Hesselbein, the CEO of Girl Scouts of the USA as a striking example of leadership in a highly diffuse power structure. "Facing a complex governance structure composed of hundreds of local Girl Scout councils (each with its own governing boards) and a volunteer force of 650,000, Hesselbein simply did not have the full power of decision" (Collins 2005, 9). Nevertheless the CEO shifted traditional Girl Scout culture by talking about tough challenges confronted by girls in the USA such as teen pregnancy and substance abuse in the organization's materials. Proficiency badges were also introduced in areas like math, technology and computer science to reinforce capabilities and diversity of career choices. While the CEO could not force these changes on local scout organizations, she made the case and left the decisions about changes to the discretion of local councils. Most of the councils decided on change.

In talking about leadership in a dispersed power structure, Hesselbein said that, "you always have power, if you just know where to find it. There is the power of inclusion and the power of language and the power of shared interests, and the power of coalition. Power is all around you to draw upon, but it is rarely raw, rarely visible" (cited by Collins 2005, 10).

The UK's Institute for Government identifies coalition building as a key success factor in implementing change initiatives, noting that the inclusion of political representation can be critical.

> Departments in which leaders worked together and shared responsibility for the change agenda were much better placed to take big strategic decisions and manage risk across silos. Where executive teams worked towards a common aim, this showed a deep-rooted commitment to change in the department. It also set an example for staff on how they should respond. This was true in the Ministry of Justice, which downsized and changed its executive team as part of building joint leadership of the Transforming Justice programmes. Ministers were generally seen to be uninterested in organizational change and, in many cases, departmental leaders were simply 'getting on with it.' However, whatever ministers' level of direct involvement, they have had a powerful influence through their words and actions. And in some departments, like the Ministry of Defence, ministers have played a pivotal role. Where we observed governance of change at its most effective, it supported leaders at the centre of departments to take collective responsibility and make joint decisions without micromanaging or burdening the implementation of individual programmes (Page, Pearson et al. 2012, 8).

Political leaders have also drawn on "guiding coalitions" to support the planning and implementation of priority initiatives. This is particularly so when change is being driven outside of a central or provincial government in the health, education and justice sectors, which are notoriously resistant to change. When first elected as Ontario's premier in 2003, Dalton McGuinty chose a small number of policy priorities but they were big ones – including reducing wait times for key health procedures, significantly improving student literacy and numeracy at the elementary level and reducing high school drop-out rates. McGuinty had closely watched Prime Minister Tony Blair experiment with a rigorous approach to implementation driven from the centre of government. With some adaptation McGuinty followed a similar course and broke with Ontario tradition in establishing powerful health and education results teams that included heavy-hitting representatives from those sectors and high profile academic experts such as Michael Fullan who has written about the importance of coalitions of teachers, parents and principals in the context of school reforms (Fullan 2006).

In his article on renewing public health care in Ontario Michael Fenn describes McGuinty's health results team (HRT), which was comprised of a mix of senior public servants and political representatives, as well as members from outside of government.

> Uniquely, it added outside experts drawn from the health care field who were charged with championing and/or validating key initiatives in the reform strategy. Leadership of the HRT was given to a senior official from British Columbia, a veteran hospital executive with extensive experience in health sector collective bargaining … One key reform portfolio (waiting times and operational performance) was led by an external leader who was a surgeon, with impeccable national, clinical and community credentials … The initiative leader for primary health care renewal (family practice physicians and front-line services) was also a prominent physician, who was a family doctor, a medical leader, and a hospital president. A third external expert led the performance measurement and data collection and analysis. He was a recognized academic expert in the complex area of health care information technology and information management (Fenn 2006, 536).

Public service and political leaders operate in a relatively rigid and rules-based environment, both in terms of governance and architecture. Their operating culture is dominated by professional and organizational silos. And yet the challenges they face are becoming more complex, boundary-less and expensive. Often missed is that public sector leaders are responsible for bridging this divide. It is evident from research and practice that building lateral networks and partnerships both inside and outside of public sector organizations is an obvious means of doing this. There are dividends in information sharing, maximizing resources, opening up policy and problem-solving processes, tackling silos and in designing and delivering effective interventions and programs. These are important practices that emerge in other chapters. It is the responsibility of leaders to assess the capacity of their organizations in these areas and to optimize them where necessary. Senior leaders must recognize the need for both hierarchical leadership and leadership that is distributed across networks.

ACCOUNTABILITY – WHO IS WEARING THE WHITE HAT?

In the hive of activity on construction sites a variety of coloured hard hats are usually evident as these are used to identify different groups of workers and to clearly identify supervisors and safety staff. If direction is required or there is a question about health and safety the site supervisor or other management personnel are quickly identifiable. Accountability is usually clear and, when it isn't, things can go wrong.

... in public servants' relationship with their political counterparts, trust and competence is demonstrated one step at a time.

Unlike on construction sites, many organizations give insufficient attention to accountability – or simply put, who is responsible for what. There are myriad reasons for this, one of which is that jobs are commonly organized by function – and functions do not necessarily line up with real-world challenges and opportunities – or with the achievement of some political priorities. Malcolm Sparrow (2000) writes about this, noting that, in the majority of award-winning regulatory innovations cited in his book, "responsibility for solving the problem did not naturally lie with any one official and had to be assigned".

In our earlier look at the delivery of health and human services in the context of the siloed architecture of government it became evident why complex needs clients fall through the cracks between service providers. This is an accountability issue. Accountability gaps can arise where an employer has not been sufficiently clear in outlining a worker or supervisor's responsibilities. Issues can also arise where some functions are similar or duplicated and, commonly, where a challenge or opportunity crosses functional or organizational boundaries. Paradoxically, some of the mechanisms put in place to advance more corporate approaches to problem solving (such as cross-ministry task groups and steering committees) can intensify accountability challenges because decisions are made to share accountability rather than resolving the tough question of which individual will be accountable for making a project successful. This occurs at the political level as well where ministers with shared accountability for delivery of a project can have competing objectives or where two or more ministers are each declaring that they are in charge.

At some stage in their career, public service managers are very likely to be asked by a senior executive, politician or senior political staffer, "Who is in charge of this project?... Who is the go-to person if I have a question?", or as I was at one point, "Who is wearing the white hat?" It's a good idea in these circumstances for executives or managers to have a clear answer ready, and preferably one that mentions just one name and one phone number. As mentioned earlier, in public servants' relationship with their political counterparts, trust and competence is demonstrated one step at a time.

As leaders take on more responsibility they need clear lines of delegation and accountability. Wherever possible, that means vesting accountability in individuals who will feel personal responsibility for delivering results – and on the plus side taking the credit for those accomplishments. Clarity of accountability is important for staff because they know where to look for direction and decisions, it is good for customers and partners because they have a single point of contact when other avenues fail and it is good for executives because they know that someone else is worrying about an important initiative and they don't have to.

THE TORONTO TRANSIT COMMISSION

Andy Byford, the CEO of the Toronto Transit Commission (TTC) under-stands this really well. When first hired he was surprised to find that there was no single person in charge of subway stations. He understands the importance of getting accountability right. Byford is a great example of a public sector leader.

> "I am incredibly proud to head up the TTC. I am quite convinced that we can get it back to being what it once was, namely the jewel in the crown of North American transit."
> —Andy Byford, CEO

The TTC is a public transport agency that operates subway, bus, streetcar and rapid transit services in Toronto, Ontario. Established in 1921, the TTC currently comprises four rapid transit lines with a total of 69 stations, as well as 181 bus routes and 11 streetcar.

The TTC operates the third most heavily used urban mass transit system in North America, after the New York City Transit Authority and Mexico City Metro. In fourth quarter 2012, the average daily ridership was 2.76 million passengers: 1,425,300 by bus, 271,100 by streetcar, 46,400 by intermediate rail, and 1,011,700 by subway. The TTC employed 12,803 personnel as of December 31, 2013.[23]

Andy Byford worked as a Station Foreman in the London Underground from 1989, rising through the ranks to become Group Station Manager of King's Cross station, the busiest station on the "Tube". Byford later moved to main line railway operations, becoming Operations and Safety Director for South Eastern Trains from 2003 to 2006 and subsequently Operations Director for sister company Southern Railway from 2006 to 2009. A Chief Operating Officer job followed with Railcorp of New South Wales, Australia. From there, Byford was hired for the same role with the TTC in November 2011. In March 2012, Byford was promoted as Chief General Manager and his role was renamed as CEO.

Byford knows the global mass transit players and had been interested in a senior job in Toronto for some time. Byford has a big day job with plenty to worry about in keeping this system running smoothly. But he takes leadership seriously; he is front and centre in dealing with bad news and emergencies, providing information and explaining what the TTC will do to put things right. Byford was on the scene shortly after a late-night shooting of a TTC ticket collector in February 2012 and when large parts of the system were shut down by severe flooding in July 2013. Despite the huge scale of his job though, it is obvious that Byford sets time aside for thinking about and implementing necessary changes.

It didn't take him long to size up what was working and not working at the TTC. But to obtain first-hand experience he spent a day at a time job shadowing a worker in each job class in the organization – including a day in a subway token booth (the TTC still sells subway and bus tokens and tickets), a shift with Transit Enforcement Officers and a day working with janitors in the TTC's Station Services division.

The CEO felt that fundamental organizational and performance issues needed to be addressed in a systematic and planned way, starting with the introduction of what he calls the "basics" of a modern performance management framework. He subsequently reorganized the TTC to focus all business activity around the customer, creating five focused business groups around a continuous improvement model designed to boost performance, customer satisfaction and company reputation.

Byford worked with his executive team to develop a vision ("A transit system that makes Toronto proud"), a suite of key performance indicators and to write a five-year Corporate Plan that acts as a road map to all employees for what needs to be done over the next five years. The TTC had not previously had such a document and it has since been presented to all 12,800 employees in a series of CEO-led Town Hall meetings to gain buy-in and understanding of what needs to be done. At the same time he recognised that asking customers to wait five years to see fundamental improvement is not acceptable. He felt, strongly, that a lot of the challenges were glaringly obvious: dirty trains, poor morale, performance management issues, a command and control management structure in which (not unusually) there was a striking absence of personal accountability and an overwhelming air of resignation in a proud organization that could not seem to break out of relentlessly bad media and embarrassing, high profile customer service failures.

Byford described it this way: "The TTC is a fantastic organization and I was lucky to inherit a lot of solid progress by my predecessor. But I felt that, for too long, mediocrity had been tolerated in the way service was delivered and presented and it seemed to me that there was a need for a 'can-do' approach to reinvigorate things. In my opinion, the staff and managers were crying out for strong leadership and a compelling vision and I set out to give them both, by showing what the TTC could be like if we all upped our game".[24]

The CEO decided to start by tackling some glaring issues that could be addressed relatively quickly, with little or no funding and yet have high visibility and value. One of these involved tackling the issue of dirty trains. Byford says he is fond of the question "Why?" And he started by asking why early morning newspapers and other trash was still on the floor of trains when commuters board for their trip home. He was told this was because trains were only cleaned at night. When he asked why that was, he was told that this was the agreement with the unions and that cleaners liked to work nights. Byford started from the premise that the status quo (dirty trains) was unacceptable so, with firm direction on what was to be achieved, cleaners were moved to terminal stations on the two principal subway lines to remove litter during the day every round trip of every train while it was still in service. Customer reaction has been positive.

Other early wins included introduction of debit and credit payment facilities at all subway ticket booths to address a long-term customer gripe that high value transactions could only be made in cash, and a fundamental overhaul of the subway's notoriously grim washrooms. Byford also oversaw development and roll-out of the TTC's inaugural Customer Charter (based on a model from both London and Sydney), a suite of 31 time-bound improvements across every aspect of TTC services.

Byford's longer term plans include addressing accountability gaps by designating single points of accountability for everything from who is in charge of a subway station to the ability of fare takers to solve problems for customers. Other areas for attention include action to improve surface transit route performance, various initiatives to drive up employee performance through improved engagement and morale and a new relationship with the unions to achieve more customer focused procedures and methods of working while keeping the TTC whole.

Andy Byford is proud of the TTC and describes it as a great organization with lots of great people. "I am incredibly proud to head up the TTC. I am quite convinced that we can get it back to being what it once was, namely the jewel in the crown of North American transit. My employees are incredibly passionate about what they do and they want the company to succeed. I have merely shown them what is possible with a refreshed approach, a clear vision and by leading by example".[25]

Byford is a terrific leader. He is friendly, approachable and hugely energetic. He wants to make a difference at the TTC and you know that he is doing that. Byford is the sort of guy you would want to work for. You would know what is important for the organization and its customers and the role you are expected to play in making that happen. He has a compelling vision of making public transit better for customers in Toronto and you trust that he will get there.

Like other CEOs, Byford doesn't operate autonomously; he reports to a transit commission chaired by a city councillor and to the city's mayor as well. But you don't hear him talking about how messy and complex this is and you certainly don't get a sense that he is second-guessed. His compelling vision makes good political sense too in view of the TTC's reputational issues. Byford is a wonderful example of leadership in the public sector.

HUMAN RESOURCES LEADERSHIP

Discussions about public service reform almost inevitably touch on the importance of human resources. Mention is commonly made about the demographics of public service organizations, recruitment and retention and building "learning organizations". The importance of the people in organizations is also routinely mentioned in major reviews and discussions of service delivery, governance and policy capacity. The reality on the ground in many public service organizations is very different – although there have been some breakthroughs in recent years, particularly in sub-national jurisdictions such as British Columbia and Ontario, both of which have developed sophisticated human resource plans.

> "HR should not be defined by what it does but by what it delivers – results that enrich the organization's value to customers, investors and employees."
> — Dave Ulrich

High level, strategic, approaches to human resources reform in the public sector are few and far between. Despite its huge importance and promise, HR is often sidelined in the landscape of public service reform. Many public service leaders communicate, but undervalue, the role of HR in business transformation. Funding in this area is often thinly or unevenly spread and the professional profile of HR executives and managers does not share the often glossy profile of their policy counterparts. This is a mistake and a missed opportunity. And yet road maps for HR reform and successful practices have been clearly laid out and are discussed at major HR conferences around the globe.

There are endless government presentations outlining the promises of stronger HR capacity. For example:

- Attracting top flight talent with an emphasis on the strength of diversity;

- Developing the incoming and existing workforce as a corporate resource with an optimal relationship bringing out the best value for the both employee and the organization (a vibrant talent management system);

- A culture that encourages employee engagement and continuous learning; and,

- A serious focus on managing performance.

The prescription is clear but is seldom fully implemented.

There are compelling reasons for action. As noted earlier public service reform is being driven by demographically-driven demands for more and better services; the scale and complexity of policy and fiscal challenges is growing and the ageing of the senior ranks of public service organizations is a looming challenge. In the Canadian federal government over 66 per cent of the public service is over 40 years of age compared to 42 per cent in 1983 and more than one-quarter of the public service is close to eligibility for full retirement. Even in the absence of this data, research shows a significant link between investment in people and organizational performance.

In their 2009, *The People Factor*, Linda Bilmes and Scott Gould (2009) make the case for a step change in thinking about human resources, arguing that the United States cannot prosper without a strong, highly functioning federal work force to manage the operations of government. The authors called for an investment of $10 billion to improve recruiting, training and management of the federal workforce predicting that investment will yield $300-$600 billion in productivity gains.

David Ulrich's earlier book, *Delivering Results*, which transformed thinking about the HR profession, makes a powerful argument for rethinking the HR profession. Ulrich calls for a radical shift away from a focus on traditional transactional services such as staffing and compensation and towards an emphasis on outcomes. "HR should not be defined by what it does but by what it delivers – results that enrich the organization's value to customers, investors and employees" (1998, 29). Ulrich says that HR professionals can contribute to organizational excellence in four ways:

- By becoming a partner with senior managers in strategy execution – moving plans to implementation;

- Developing expertise in the way work is organized and executed to help drive down costs while maintaining quality;

- Becoming a champion for employees, representing their concerns to senior management while increasing employee contribution and commitment to the organization and their ability to deliver results; and

- HR should be an agent of continuous transformation, shaping processes and developing a culture that improves the organization's capacity for change (1998, 30).

The Office of Personnel Management in the United States was an early adopter of Ulrich's model. Canadian initiatives, predominantly developed in British Columbia and Ontario are also influenced by Ulrich's work. The UK's focus on talent management, developing strategies for addressing poor performers, succession planning, leadership, employee engagement and the development of performance measures for HR will be familiar to many Canadian practitioners.

A number of HR leaders have taken Ulrich's rallying cry to heart, as have some public service leaders. The scale of the UK's public sector HR challenge is considerable. The central government sector in England and Wales comprises close to half a million workers (excluding the armed forces). Early in his tenure, former UK Cabinet Secretary Gus O'Donnell and I talked about the importance of putting HR on the front burner and my advice was that he might well have to go beyond the normal civil service pay scale in order to attract the leadership talent to make that happen. Following an external recruitment for a Director General for Leadership and People Strategy in the Cabinet Office, O'Donnell hired Gill Rider, a twenty-seven-year veteran of consulting firm Accenture, who had risen to the role of Chief Global Leadership Officer. Rider said O'Donnell asked her to focus on three main areas. "He's asked me to help him develop the next generation of leaders for the civil service; to create a people strategy for the civil service, and to improve the HR organizations across the civil service" (Dean 2009, 15-16). Rider said that the Cabinet Secretary sees all three objectives as levers that can be pulled to help make change happen. Rider also had executive responsibility for capability reviews. In another early signal of an intention to raise the profile of HR, O'Donnell invited Rider to join meetings of the permanent secretary cadre, where she sat at his right hand. Rider's size-up of the HR profession was frank, emphasizing that HR did not currently understand what business it is in, that the profession had to earn respect at executive tables and also had to appreciate how all the parts of HR fit together to get to desired outcomes (Dean 2009, 15-17).

Prior to Rider's appointment in the UK, and in very similar circumstances, I determined that Ontario's public service needed more strength in human resources leadership. I was convinced that stronger HR capacity would contribute to delivering on my priorities for organizational change, which included developing a stronger and more integrated culture of service delivery, breaking down organizational silos, developing more integrated approaches to policy development and implementation. As a result, Michelle DiEmanuele, a former Ontario public service executive who had moved to an executive HR role in a major Canadian bank, was recruited back to the Ontario Public Service as Associate Secretary of Cabinet and Deputy Minister to lead that organization's HR renewal effort. DiEmanuele knew the organization well and understood its challenges. She returned to the public service with considerable private sector experience and a strong mandate to transform the role of HR from the local unit level up to the deputy ministers' council.

Dave Ulrich would like Michelle DiEmanuele. She introduced an employee engagement survey to assess the degree of commitment of staff to the organization and to learn about what staff need from the organization. The initial results were sobering but established an important benchmark from which to assess progress. I particularly recall the survey highlighting a need for more open communications from managers and leaders. Over time, this survey has provided more granular data at the ministry level which provides for analysis of significant variations in results between ministries. In parallel, a human resources "balanced scorecard' was used to measure key indicators for human resources services and costs such as recruitment time and spending on training, both of which varied widely by location.

DiEmanuele also introduced a recruitment modernization strategy, established a diversity office and a unit focused on the recruitment and retention of both young and new professional entrants (led by young professionals). The diversity strategy is crucial. Ontario has one of the most diverse populations on the globe and yet that diversity is not reflected in the demographics of Ontario's public service, and certainly not in the leadership ranks of public and private sector organizations. A number of diversity initiatives followed including one which saw deputy ministers identifying high-potential candidates in their organizations for mentoring and candidacy for developmental opportunities. A new HR delivery model was introduced, which provided support on strategy to senior managers and deputy ministers and tailored support to middle managers in areas of need identified by that cadre. Recruitment processing time was reduced by 50 per cent and a northern recruitment strategy put in place to address difficulties in attracting professional staff.

A revamped and rigorous "talent management" and succession planning process was developed to improve the organization's performance in aligning talent with organizational objectives. This included advance mapping of hard-to-fill jobs and the designation of potential candidates with an associated assessment of development needs. Work in this area included a more sophisticated approach to the recruitment of deputy ministers, including benchmarking of internal and external candidates by professional recruitment firms. These approaches brought to life Collins and Kotter's call to "get the right people on the bus" and the right people promoted to the right positions.

For a long time, the modernization of the HR function had been hampered by decades-old public service legislation. With a push from me and support from the premier, legislation was developed and passed which amended the governance structure in place for managing promotions and succession planning for senior positions. The amendments also strengthened the principles guiding the work of public servants: accountability, non-partisan professionalism and competency. In addition, the amendments clarified the respective roles and accountabilities of public servants in relation to political staff. Progress on these reforms was captured in an annual report from the organization's Public Service Commission.

DiEmanuele also understood the importance of HR strategy in supporting organizational priorities. A year or so into her mandate she was given additional responsibility for ServiceOntario and for corporate information technology services. Oversight over HR and IT, which she understood as critical change levers, as well as having a crow's nest view of organizational talent allowed DiEmanuele to drive towards one of the organization's top priorities: the reduction of costs and improvement of customer services by moving high-volume services to online channels. She was highly successful in doing this, especially in the area of business registrations and applications for birth certificates, the latter of which was accompanied by a money-back service guarantee (described earlier in Chapter 8).

HR STRATEGY AND LABOUR RELATIONS

The portfolio of human resources leaders normally includes managing labour relations, which tend to ebb and flow with the cadence of economic conditions (Swimmer and Bartkiw 2003). Post-2008 financial constraints and increasing demands for services have combined to exert considerable strain on management-union relationships. In a heavily-unionized public sector, with about 70 per cent union density, this quickly finds its way to bargaining tables. This is especially so today because employee compensation represents over 50 per cent of public sector program spending.

In 2013-14, Canada's federal government intervened with legislation to prevent several strikes, including one at Air Canada, a federally regulated air carrier. In the same timeframe, British Columbia and Ontario were locked in bitter struggles with teachers' unions, which in Ontario was prompted by legislated changes to collective agreements to curb the cost of benefits. Drummond (2012) and others have suggested that governments move away from wage freezes and across-the-board job cuts, promoting instead a "program review" approach based on evaluating public services on their efficiency and effectiveness, and eliminating duplication through integration and consolidation.

If governments as funders are becoming more muscular, so are unions. The Ontario Public Service Employees Union (OPSEU) fought back against contracting out in the mid-late 1990s period of Conservative government, following contracted-out work and re-unionizing staff. OPSEU has more recently campaigned for curbs on privatization and contracting out (Ontario Public Service Employees Union 2013). And on the legal front, the Supreme Court of Canada has arguably expanded collective bargaining rights in curbing unilateral efforts by government to legislate changes to collective agreements. In February 2014, an Alberta Court upheld an injunction launched by the Alberta Union of Public Employees which has stalled government legislation that would have imposed terms and conditions of the collective agreement (OHS Canada 2014).

While the government of British Columbia has some major labour relations challenges, it has been successful in bargaining protocols on contracting out with its public sector unions. These provide for an employment offer, the same or better pay and benefits and pension coverage, and retention of union membership. The UK and New Zealand have similar frameworks in place. OPSEU has promoted a five-point Public Service Protection Plan as a decision-making template (Hjartarson, McGuinty and Schwenger 2014).

It is clear that status quo approaches to public sector bargaining, which are still informed by processes and behaviours developed in an era of industrial labour relations, are unresponsive to rapidly changing circumstances and pressures. Without some form of change the rules of the game are going to be determined by the courts or strikes and lockouts. These pathways are expensive, turbulent and counter-productive and are likely to result in a decline in workplace relations, together with a negative impact on the quality of public services.

At the very least, more proactive dialogue and transparency is required of governments and employers, with an earnest effort being made to share the details of financial pressures and draft business plans. This should not just be aligned with collective bargaining cycles, when emotions are running high. It should be an ongoing activity. Public sector union leaders are, for the most part, skilful and sophisticated and would likely welcome this sort of opportunity. This dialogue should be nurtured on all sides. Just like the work of public servants, trust must be built one step at a time, with a focus on tackling big challenges and opportunities. A recent example is the new *School Boards Collective Bargaining Act* in Ontario, which was based on a high degree of consensus among the parties about an amended bargaining process. This includes the direct involvement of the government with the school board employers and unions in bargaining and a two-tiered process with central and local matters being determined at separate bargaining tables.

Protocols outlining employee rights in organizational change initiatives are proving useful in some jurisdictions and should be closely monitored for potential adoption. But for the longer term, it is likely time for a thorough and impartial review of public sector labour relations in Canada with a view to examining options for adaptation to the very different social, economic and legal environment that is unfolding in Canada's public sector.

ACCELERATING INNOVATION IN THE PUBLIC SECTOR[26]

There are clarion calls in many governments around the world for greater innovation in the public sector and a parallel growth in literature focused on the public sector (Eggers and Macmillan 2013; Bourgon 2011; Bason 2010). Moreover, innovation is increasingly critical and urgent as public servants work to improve the quality and efficiency of public services in response to quickly-changing social and economic conditions. Tough policy challenges abound in social services, addressing poverty, finding the right balance between environmental protection and resource development, and responding to physical and

There are thousands of innovations in public services at every level but most of them stay below the radar.

mental health challenges to name just a few. Breakthroughs in these areas requires new ideas and approaches, especially in a context of surging demand, declining revenues, and a political focus on delivering measurable outcomes.

Innovation involves doing new things or doing existing things differently. It also goes hand in hand with experimentation which by its nature involves trial and, sometimes, error. But "error" doesn't fit well in risk-averse environments where there is little tolerance for failure or in organizations that are resistant to change, as is the case in many public service organizations (Public Policy Forum 1998). There are thousands of innovations in public services at every level but most of them stay below the radar. Nevertheless, a common question at most staff meetings and planning retreats is, "How can we innovate more when there is so little appetite for risk and tolerance for mistakes?" Leaders owe their staff an answer. So how can we break through this challenge to innovate faster and to replicate or adapt the innovations already happening in public sector organizations?

As a start, managers and front-line staff would benefit from a clear understanding of what innovation means in their organization, a clear message from the top of the organization about the degree of freedom they have to innovate, and step-by-step advice on the application of risk identification and risk mitigation to innovative projects. While risk aversion is common in public sector organizations, it is not a significant deterrent to innovation in all jurisdictions – it is simply one of the factors to be addressed in establishing an environment in which innovation can flourish. As noted previously, public servants are innovating already, both in developing polices and designing and implementing programs – but the success stories, how they were accomplished and the lessons learned are not being sufficiently shared.

Experience in Canada and other jurisdictions suggests that progress in promoting innovation, while managing risk to the extent possible, requires leadership in at least three areas:

- Learning from close-to-home innovations in our own organizations and sectors (as well as others). Formalizing knowledge capture and a means of effectively sharing it, shining a spotlight on successful pilots and supporting communities of practice. This connects to human resources strategies designed to build learning organizations.

- Providing necessary support and tools to ongoing innovation projects. This includes an explanation of what "innovation" means in the context of a particular organization, outlining clear expectations, providing training and support in managing risk and employing data to monitor implementation in real time.

- Connecting innovation to organizational objectives and priorities, and the broader transformation agenda. There is also another point of crossover here to human resource strategies focusing on organizational renewal, culture change, incentives, and a focus on results.

The chart below unpacks this in a little more detail. There are a few key messages here. First, significant change will require sustained leadership, modeled behavior, and culture change. This includes explicit permission for managers to innovate, providing tools and frameworks for risk identification and mitigation and the empowerment of front-line professionals. Second, this bridges to efforts being made by many of Canada's public service leaders to bring a more strategic approach to the practice of human resource development and to break down entrenched departmental, ministry and professional silos. Third, high-level political support should be sought for a step-by-step innovation agenda. Exemplary public service initiatives usually reflect well on the government of the day, regardless of its political stripe.

Successful innovations can be highlighted and support built for scaled experimental pilots with an emphasis on risk mitigation, real-time monitoring and recognition of the possible need for course correction or termination. Sometimes programs do not work out well and it's important to know that before they become entrenched. Last but not least, while it is important to look around the world for best practices, the most important ones are those closest to home. It is vital that these be identified and disseminated, and that communities of innovative practitioners are supported and rewarded.

THREE LEADERSHIP STRATEGIES TO FOSTER INNOVATION

Innovation Capture and Dissemination	Leadership Support for Projects	Leadership at the Organizational Level
• Set in place formal mechanisms for organizational knowledge capture and dissemination. • Spotlight successful innovations and what has been learned from failure. • Senior management sponsorship and support for communities of practice – buttressed by corporate communications. • HR engagement strategies focus on encouraging innovative ideas and practices at the front-line. • A learning culture helps to scale-up and replicate innovation. Increase cross-jurisdictional dissemination of successful innovation.	• Outline clear expectations but leave room for innovation. • Ensure focus on early identification of potential risks, data-driven monitoring and mitigation strategies; managers and staff must understand what this means and have the tools and capacity to get it done. • Use of pilots with careful evaluation and rapid feedback loops – and willingness to shut down project if not working – and learn from that. • Potentially learn from modern risk management practices in the regulatory sphere.	• Promoting innovation, actions to overcome cultural and organizational barriers (e.g., silos), and ensuring consistent risk management practices. • Clarify organizational objectives and priorities and where innovation fits in: what success looks like. • Recognize innovation as part of the broader transformation agenda (HR renewal, learning organization, incentives, focus on results). • Obtain political support for desired direction and associated culture change. Focus on government priorities and mutually beneficial pilots.

CONCLUSIONS

This chapter has explored leadership in the public sector in the broader context of reforming and improving public sector organizations. It discusses the relatively low profile of leadership in the public sector and makes the case for more conscious and activist forms of leadership in public organizations. Key aspects of this emerging profile include finding an appropriate balance between preserving important values and driving necessary changes; establishing priorities and a compelling vision; and, building coalitions and driving change from the top of the organization while providing explicit permission to change-ready staff and managers to innovate at all levels of the organization.

Leadership in the public service lies in finding a balance between day-to-day management of operations and transformational change.

I also argue for the elevation of human resources management and strategy in view of its important, yet still underdeveloped, contribution to capacity building, culture change, performance management and employee engagement. It reminds us that HR strategy also extends to other critical areas of public sector activity, including collective bargaining and building more innovative organizations.

At the heart of the chapter is a reminder of the accountability of public service leaders in building and leading high performance public service organizations, equipped to support the government with sound and non-partisan professional advice and with the capacity to provide the best possible services to citizens at an affordable price. This is becoming more pressing in view of the complexity of the fiscal and policy challenges confronting governments and increasing citizen expectations of public services.

Patrice Dutil has asked an important question about whether public service leadership involves the day-to-day management of operations, making incremental course corrections where necessary, or whether the mandate of leaders extends to transformational change. The case is made here that leadership in the public sector involves finding the right balance between the two. In view of the challenges and complexities in the public sector, building a strong, capable and committed workforce, elevating human resources strategies to executive tables, breaking down policy, fiscal and service delivery silos between ministries and agencies to ensure the best results for citizens, and delivering top-flight advice and support to elected governments would collectively be transformational enough for most public sector organizations.

ADVICE FOR GOVERNMENTS, LEADERS AND PRACTITIONERS

- Political and public service leaders would benefit from discussing what is expected from the public service in relation to reform of public administration and service delivery. Political leaders should also consider the extent to which they wish to play a more active role in shaping directions in public administration reforms beyond discussion about compensation and benefits;

- Leaders at all levels of public sector organizations should think seriously about leadership practice in the context of the governance system in which they operate. The conscious practice of leadership requires dedicated time and effort. It is not an "add-on" job. A frank evaluation of the capacity of the work unit, team, department or ministry to deliver successfully on its mandate is a critical first step, followed by the selection of a small number of priorities to address issues, or take advantage of opportunities, with an emphasis on what will bring the highest value for the government, citizens and service users. As these are communicated to the organization, staff and managers will benefit from a clear sense of what is important in the organization and what the vision or end result (success) looks like;

- Public service leaders are responsible for bridging the divide between the relatively rigid, siloed, and rules-based environment in which they operate internally and the complex, boundary-less and networked environment they must engage with externally. Working across boundaries sharing information, defining challenges, and designing policy and program interventions in collaboration with partners and service users should become the norm. These are important practices that emerge in other chapters. It is the responsibility of leaders to assess the capacity of their organizations in these areas and to provide strong leadership and incentives where necessary;

- Establishing networks within and across organizational boundaries is helpful in obtaining support for corporate change initiatives, but it is also important to provide explicit permission to change activists in pre-existing networks to both innovate locally and support corporate change initiatives;

- Prioritizing a small number of problem areas in the organization and fixing them quickly helps to build organizational momentum;

- Leadership is about the big picture but is also about small but powerful gestures of thanks or commiseration. Authenticity, humility and honesty are powerful attributes. Managers and staff monitor leaders' behaviour constantly and in many cases emulate their values and attributes;

- The transformation of human resources strategy and delivery is a foundational element of public service reform. It should be front and centre and be given "parity of esteem" with other public service professions. This requires the best possible transformational leadership and if this talent is not available internally it should be found externally;

- There should be a sustained focus on building capacity for tackling complex and cross-cutting policy challenges with a focus on "boundary spanning skills". Emerging skills include an ability to access multiple data sources rapidly for decision makers, communications, negotiation, and problem solving skills, networking and collaboration, procurement and contract management, and policy, strategy and implementation skills;

- Organizational skill development should focus on leadership and strategy, attracting and developing talent, evidence-driven and more open policy-making, connecting across boundaries, implementation

informed by data and engaging staff in policy development and public
service renewal efforts;

- The recent focus on employee engagement and maximizing the opportunities of diversity should be accelerated and intensified;

- It would be advisable for government and public service leaders to
reconsider industrial-era approaches to labour-management relations
and collective bargaining. Key elements of this should be an increased
emphasis on transparency, data sharing and the thinking behind organizational changes that will have an impact on staff. Advance notice of
potential change initiatives with timely opportunities to comment and
offer alternatives are building blocks for more positive relationships.
More broadly, consideration should be given to a review of public sector
collective bargaining in Canada;

- Last, in view of the importance of innovation in building high performance public sector organizations, leaders should: ensure that innovative practices are being captured and shared; that expectations and key
concepts are clearly outlined; and, that innovation is connected to organizational objectives and priorities.

CHAPTER 9
CONCLUDING OBSERVATIONS

A QUICK RECAP

This book explores interconnections and synergies between new forms of policy development, public service delivery, and human resources management through the lens of case studies, reports, and the author's own experience in government. We began by describing some of the major pressures confronting governments and public sector organizations, and by exploring their siloed and fragmented architecture and cultures. This is followed with a look at governments' efforts to respond to these external pressures by reforming, reshaping and working around their own organizational architecture and processes for policy-making and service delivery.

BIG TRENDS

The substantive chapters in the book examine integrated approaches to policy design and development; the implementation of major political priorities; integrated service delivery both at the transactional level and in the more complex world of human services; and the often-controversial field of alternative service delivery. These changes reflect an increasing shift from an insular view of government "knowing best", to one which attempts to design public services and their delivery from citizens and service users' perspectives. This requires engagement with users and citizens, resulting in more informed policy-making and more responsive and relevant services. These changes have been prompted in part by governments' loss of hegemony over information and ideas, partly caused by the democratization of data enabled by digitization and the Internet. Thus, governments are now turning to technology as part of a shift to more open policy-making, integrated online citizen service delivery, and integrated patient and client records in the health and community services sectors. All of these initiatives have, or support, a new focus on the citizen as a client of government services.

COMMON DENOMINATORS

Some common elements across reform initiatives are evident. To some degree these reflect:

- a changing relationship between citizens and the state;

- working across silos through collaboration and integration in both policy-making and service delivery (both inside and outside of government);

- a shift from a focus on inputs to a focus on measurable results; and,

- the importance of appropriate governance and accountability.

In turn, all are reliant on enablers such as the application of rigorous data and evidence, high-level strategic human resources leadership, new technology and, above all, top-level public service leadership. We also touch on the more recent interest in tackling siloed funding streams and the disintermediation of currently complex policy "supply chains" in an effort to develop a straighter and shorter line from a government priority or funder to the intended recipient of a government service.

THE CLOSING POINT

In view of the enormous complexity involved in working in the public sector and the advanced navigational skills that are necessary to do that well, the issues and opportunities discussed in this book are relatively straightforward. Bringing a citizen perspective to the design of policy and delivery mechanisms is a democratic imperative. Building networked and collaborative services in ways that wrap around multiple-needs clients will close the gaps that vulnerable people otherwise fall through. Assessing the capacity and skills needed by governments and building that capacity is a foundational element of public service reform. And we need leaders to lead, even if that takes a somewhat different character in the public sector.

If public service organizations can find a way to do this small number of things really well and harvest the synergies between them, they will optimize the services they provide to citizens and elected governments. They will become stronger, more adaptive and resilient, and will be well-positioned to accomplish great things.

We should expect no less.

SELECTED BIBLIOGRAPHY

Accenture. 2007. *Leadership in Customer Service: Delivering on the Promise.* http://nstore.accenture.com/acn_com/PDF/2007LCSDelivPromise Final.pdf

Agronoff, Robert and Michael McGuire. 2001. "Big Questions in Public Network Management Research." *Journal of Public Administration Research and Theory* 11:3: 295-326.

--2003. *Collaborative Public Management: New Strategies for Local Governments.* Washington, DC: Georgetown University Press.

Alberta Ministry of Human Services. 2013. .

Alford, John and Owen Hughes. 2008. "Public Value Pragmatism as the Next Phase of Public Management." *American Review of Public Administration* 38:130-48.

Ambrose, Rona. 2011. Creation of Shared Services Canada: Speaking Notes for the Honourable Rona Ambrose, Minister of Public Works and Government Services and Minister for the Status of Women. Ottawa. August 4, 2011. Accessed at .

Asselin, Robert B. 2001. Political and Social Affairs Division – Library of Parliament; 18 January 2001. Accessed at .

Aucoin, Peter. 1990. "Administrative Reform in Public Management: Paradigms, Principles, Paradoxes and Pendulums." *Governance* 3 (2): 115-37.

--1995. *The New Public Management: Canada in Comparative Perspective.* Montreal: Institute for Research on Public Policy.

Auditor General of Canada. 1993. *Report of the Auditor General of Canada to the House of Commons.* Ottawa: Ministry of Supply and Services.

--2005. "Managing horizontal initiatives." *Report of the Auditor General of Canada to the House of Commons* (Chapter 4). November 2005. Ottawa: Minister of Public Works and Government Services Canada.

Barber, Michael. 2007. *Instruction to Deliver: Tony Blair, Public Services and the Challenge of Achieving Targets.* London: Portico.

Bardach, E. 1998. *Getting Agencies to Work Together: The Practice and Theory of Managerial Craftsmanship.* Washington, DC: The Brookings Institution.

Barnard, Chester. 1938. *The Functions of the Executive.* Cambridge: Harvard University Press.

Bason, Christian. 2010. *Leading Public Sector Innovation: Co-creating for a Better Society.* Bristol: The Policy Press.

Bass, Bernard M. 1998. *Transformational Leadership: Industrial, Military and Educational Impact.* London: Laurence Erlbaum Associates.

Batley, Richard. 1996. "Public-Private Relationships and Performance in Service Provision." *Urban Studies* 33 (4-5): 723-51.

Bel, Germa and Mildred Warner. 2008. "Challenging issues in local privatization." *Environment and Planning C: Government and Policy* 26(1): 104-109.

Bhatnagar, Subhash. 2014. *Public service delivery: Role of information and communication technology in improving governance and development impact.* Manila: Asian Development Bank.

Bilmes, Linda and Scott Gould. 2009. *The People Factor: Strengthening America by Investing in Public Service.* Washington, DC: Brookings Institution Press.

Blatchford, Kate and Tom Gash. 2012. *Commissioning for success: How to avoid the pitfalls of open public services.* London: Institute for Government.

Bognador, V., ed. 2005. *Joined-Up Government.* Oxford: Oxford University Press.

Borins, Sandford. 2002. "New Public Management, North American Style." In *New Public Management: Current Trends and Future Prospects.* Edited by Kate McLaughlin, Stephen P. Osborne and Ewan Ferlie, 181-94. London: Routledge.

Bourgault, Jacques. 2008. "Clerks and Secretaries to Cabinet: Anatomy of Leadership." In *Searching for Leadership: Secretaries to Cabinet in*

Canada. Edited by Patrice Dutil, 41-81. Toronto: University of Toronto Press.

Bourgon, Jocelyne. 2009. *Program Review: The Government of Canada's experience eliminating the deficit, 1994-99.* London: Institute for Government.

--2011. *A New Synthesis of Public Administration: Serving in the 21st Century.* Montreal: McGill-Queen's University Press,

Boutilier, Marie and Robin Mason. 2012. "The Reflexive Practitioner in Health Promotion: From Reflection to Reflexivity." In *Health Promotion in Canada: Critical Perspectives.* Edited by Rootman, Irving, Sophie Dupéré, Ann Pederson, and Michel O'Neill. 2007. Revised, 3rd ed., 2012. 196-208. Toronto: Canadian Scholars' Press Inc.

Brown, Kerry and Jennifer Waterhouse. 2013. "Managing the Change Process: The State of the Art." In *Handbook of Innovation in Public Services,* edited by Stephen P. Osborne and Louise Brown, 107-17. Cheltenham: Edward Elgar.

Cabinet Office. 2008. *Excellence and Fairness: Achieving World Class Public Services.* London: Crown Copyright.

-- 2010. Policy *Paper: Building the Big Society.*

-- 2011. *Policy Paper: Open Public Services.* Accessed at www.gov.uk/government/publications/open-public-services-white-paper

Canadian Council for Public-Private Partnerships. 2010. *Building Canada's Future: Canadian Attitudes to Public-Private Partnerships, 2004-2010.* Toronto: Council.

Canadian Union of Public Employees. 2014. *Fact Sheet: Clean, Safe and Public Water Services.* Accessed at cupe.ca/municipalities/clean-safe-public-water-services.

Casey, L. 2012. *Listening to Troubled Families: A report by Louise Casey, CB.* United Kingdom: Department for Local Communities and Government.

Castells, Manuel. 1996. *The Rise of the Network Society. (The Information Age: Economy, Society and Culture, Volume 1).* Second Ed., 2009. Malden, MA: Blackwell Publishers, Inc.

Chew, Celine and Fergus Lyon. 2013. "Social Enterprise and Innovation in Third Sector Organizations." In *Handbook of Innovation in Public Services,* edited by Stephen P. Osborne and Louise Brown, 107-17. Cheltenham, UK: Edward Elgar.

Chrislip, David D., and Carl E. Larson. 1994. *Collaborative Leadership: How Citizens and Civic Leaders Can Make a Difference*. San Francisco: Jossey-Bass Publishers.

Clerk of the Privy Council. 2011. *Eighteenth Annual Report to the Prime Minister on the Public Service of Canada*. Ottawa: Privy Council Office.

—2014. *Destination 2020*. Ottawa: Privy Council Office. Accessed at http://www.clerk.gc.ca/local_grfx/d2020/Destination2020-eng.pdf

Collins, James C. 2001. *Good to Great: Why Some Companies Make the Leap – and Others Don't*. New York: Harper Business.

—2005. *Good to Great and the Social Sectors*. Boulder, Colorado: Jim Collins.

Deber, Raisa. 2002. *Delivering Health Care Services: Public, Not-for-Profit, or Private?* Discussion Paper No.17. Ottawa: Commission on the Future of Health Care in Canada.

Dean, Tony. 2009. *U.K. Public Service Reforms: A Canadian Perspective*. Toronto: The Institute of Public Administration in Canada.

—2011. "Is Public Service Delivery Obsolete?" *Literary Review of Canada*. September 2011.

Dean, Tony and Marie Boutilier. 2012. *Joint Service Delivery in Federations*. Ottawa: The Forum of Federations.

Denis, Jean-Louis, Ann Langley, and Linda Rouleau. 2005. "Rethinking Leadership in Public Organizations." In *The Oxford Handbook of Public Management*, edited by Ewan Ferlie, Laurence E. Lynne Jr. and Christopher Pollitt, 446-467. Oxford: Oxford University Press.

Department for Communities and Local Government. 2013. *Working with Troubled Families: A guide to the evidence and good practice*. London: Department for Communities and Local Government.

Dobel, J. Patrick. 2005. "Public Management as Ethics." In *The Oxford Handbook of Public Management*. Edited by Ewan Ferlie, Laurence E. Lynn, and Christopher Pollitt, 27-50. Oxford: Oxford University Press.

Downs, Anthony. 1967. *Inside Bureaucracy*. Boston: Little, Brown and Company.

Drucker, Peter F. "What Makes an Effective Executive." *Harvard Business Review* June 2004; 82(6): 58-63.

Drummond, Don. 2012. *Public Services for Ontarians: A Path to Sustainability and Excellence*. Commission on the Reform of Ontario's Public Services. Toronto: Queen's Printer for Ontario.

––2013 "Drummond report's author gives Ontario budget a 'B'". *Globe and Mail*, May 3, 2013.

Duncan, Dwight. 2012. *Strong Action for Ontario: 2012 Ontario Budget. Provincial Budget,* Toronto: Queen's Printer for Ontario.

Dunleavy, Patrick. 1985. "Bureaucrats, Budgets and the Growth of the State." *British Journal of Political Science* 15: 299-328.

––2010. *The Future of Joined-up Public Services.* London: 2020 Public Services Trust.

Dunleavy, Patrick and Christopher Hood. 1994. "From Old Public Management to New Public Management." *Public Money and Management* 14:9-16.

Dunleavy, Patrick, Helen Margetts, Simon Bastow, and Jane Tinkler. 2006. "New Public Management is Dead—Long Live Digital-Era Governance." *Journal of Public Administration Research and Theory* 16:3: 467-94.

Dutil, Patrice, ed. 2008. *Searching for Leadership: Secretaries to Cabinet in Canada.* Toronto: University of Toronto Press.

––Dutil, Patrice. 2008. "Searching for Leadership." In *Searching for Leadership: Secretaries to Cabinet in Canada,* edited by Patrice Dutil 13-40. Toronto: University of Toronto Press.

Economist. 2012. "Searching for Dave." *The Economist,* July 21-27, 2012.

Eggars, William D., and Paul Macmillan. 2013. *The Solution Revolution: How Business, Government and Social Enterprises are Teaming Up to Solve Society's Toughest Problems.* Boston: Harvard Business Review Press.

Eggers, William D., and John O'Leary. 2009. *If We Can Put a Man on the Moon: Getting Big Things Done in Government.* Boston: Harvard Business Press.

English, Bill. 2011. "The 'new responsibility model' for New Zealand public-sector CEOs" in *Delivering Policy Reform: Anchoring Significant Reforms in Turbulent Times.* Edited by Evert A. Lindquist, Sam Vincent and John Wanna. 53-64. Canberra: ANU E-Press.

Expert Advisory Panel on Occupational Health and Safety. 2010. *Report and Recommendations to the Minister of Labour.* Toronto: Ontario Ministry of Labour.

Farneti, Federica, Emanuele Padovani, and David W. Young. 2010. "Governance of Outsourcing and Contractual Relationships." In *The New Public Governance: Emerging Perspectives on the Theory and Practice of Public Governance.* Edited by Stephen P. Osborne, 255-69. Abingdon, Oxfordshire: Routledge.

Fenn, Michael. 2006. "Reinvigorating Publicly Funded Healthcare in Ontario: New Public Policy and Public Administration Techniques." *Canadian Public Administration.* Vol. 49, No. 4, Winter 2006: 527-547.

---2014. *Recycling Ontario's Assets: A New Framework for Managing Public Finances.* Mowat Research 85. Toronto: Mowat Centre, University of Toronto.

Fenna, Alan. 2010. *Benchmarking in Federal Systems.* Occasional Paper Series Number 6. Ottawa: The Forum of Federations.

Ferlie, Ewan, Laurence E. Lynne Jr, and Christopher Pollitt, eds. 2005. *The Oxford Handbook of Public Management.* Oxford: Oxford University Press.

Flaherty, James. 2012. *Jobs, Growth and Long-Term Prosperity: Economic Action Plan 2012.* Ottawa: Public Works and Government Service Canada.

Frederickson, H. George, and Kevin B. Smith. 2003. *The Public Administration Theory Primer.* Boulder: Westview.

Fullan, Michael. 2006. *Turnaround Leadership.* San Francisco: Jossey Bass.

Galley, Andrew, Jennier Gold and Sunil Johal. 2013. *Public Service Transformed: Harnessing the Power of Behavioural Insights.* Toronto: Mowat Centre, University of Toronto.

Gash, Tom, Nehal Panchamia, Sam Sims, and Louisa Hotson. 2013. *Making Public Service Markets Work.* London: Institute for Government.

Gershon, Peter. 2004. *Releasing Resources to the Front-line: Independent Review of Public Sector Efficiency.* London: Her Majesty's Treasury.

Gold, Jennifer and Nevena Dragicevic. 2013. *The Integration Imperative: reshaping the delivery of human and social services.* Toronto: KPMG and the Mowat Centre, University of Toronto.

Gold, Jennifer with Josh Hjartarson. 2012. *Integrating Human Services in an Age of Fiscal Restraint: A Shifting Gears Report.* Toronto: Mowat Centre, University of Toronto. Supported by KPMG.

Gold, Jennifer, Matthew Mendelsohn, and Josh Hjartarson. 2011. *Fiscal Sustainability and the Future of Public Services: A Shifting Gears Progress Report.* Toronto: Mowat Centre, University of Toronto. Supported by KPMG.

Goldsmith, Stephen and William D. Eggers. 2004. *Governing by Network: The New Shape of the Public Sector*. Washington, DC: Brookings Institution Press.

Government of Ontario. 2004. *Canada-Ontario Memorandum of Agreement on Collaboration in the Delivery of Public Service*. Archived backgrounder first published on May 13, 2004. Accessed at http://news.ontario.ca/opo/en/2004/05/canada---ontario-memorandum-of-agreement-on-collaboration-in-the-delivery-of-public-service.html.

Gulick, Luther. 1937. *Papers on the Science of Administration*. New York: Institute of Public Administration.

Haldane, Richard. 1918. *Report of the Machinery of Government Committee under the chairmanship of Viscount Haldane of Cloan*. London: Her Majesty's Stationery Office.

Hallsworth, Michael and Jill Rutter. 2011. *Making Policy Better: Improving Whitehall's Core Business*. London: Institute for Government.

Head, Brian. 2008. "Three Lenses of Evidence-Based Policy." *Australian Journal of Public Administration*, 67 (1): 1-11.

--2010. *Reconsidering Evidence-Based Policy: Key Issues and Challenges*. Policy and Society , 29: 77-94.

--2013. "Evidence-Based Policy-Making for Innovation." In *Handbook of Innovation in Public Services* edited by Stephen P. Osborne and Louise Brown, 107-17. Cheltenham: Edward Elgar.

Hebdon Robert, and Patrice Jalette. 2008. "The restructuring of municipal services: a Canada – United States comparison." *Environment and Planning C: Government and Policy*, 26(1): 144-158.

Heintzman, Ralph. 2006. "Public Service Values and Ethics: From Principles to Results." *Canadian Government Executive*. Vol.12, no. 1: 10-13.

Himelfarb, Alex and Jordan Himelfarb, eds. 2013. *Tax is Not a Four-Letter Word: A Different Take on Taxes in Canada*. Waterloo: Wilfred Laurier University Press.

Hjartarson, Josh, Liam McGuinty, and Alexandra Schwenger. 2014. *Unlocking the Public Service Economy in Ontario: A New Approach to Public-Private Partnership in Services*. Toronto: Ontario Chamber of Commerce.

Hodge, Graeme. 2000. *Privatization: An International Review of Performance*. Boulder: Westview Press.

Hood, Christopher. 1991. "A Public Management for All Seasons." *Public Administration*, 69:1, Spring: 3-19.

House of Commons Public Administration Select Committee. 2011. *Role of the head of the Civil Service*. Oral Evidence taken before the Public Administration Committee, Parliament, United Kingdom. Tuesday 15 November 2011.

--2012. *Leadership of change: new arrangements for the roles of the Head of the Civil Service and the Cabinet Secretary*. Nineteenth Report of Session 2010-12. London: The Stationery Office Limited.

Hughes, Owen. 2003. *Public Management and Administration: An Introduction* (3rd ed.) Basingstoke: Palgrave/Macmillan.

Huxham, Chris, ed. 1996. *Creating Collaborative Advantage*. London: Sage Publications Ltd.

--2000. *Public-Private Partnerships: Theory and Practice in International Perspective*. London: Routledge.

Huxham, Chris and Siv Vangan. 2000. "What Makes Partnerships Work." In *Public-Private Partnerships*, 293-310, edited by Stephen P. Osborne. London: Routledge.

Ingraham, Patricia Wallace, and Heather G. Taylor. 2003. "Leadership in the Public Sector: Models and Assumptions for Leadership Development in the Federal Government." Paper presented to the Midwest Political Science Association National Conference, April 2003.

Institute for Citizen-Centred Service. 2005. *Citizens First 4*. Toronto: Institute for Citizen-Centred Service.

--2008. "Canadians Say Good Service Matters." News release. . Accessed on April 6, 2015.

Institute for Government. 2011. *Transformation in the Ministry of Justice: Interim Evaluation Report*. London: Institute for Government.

Jarvis, M.D. 2014. "Hierarchical Accountability." In *The Oxford Handbook of Public Accountability*, 405–420), edited by M. Bovens, R. Goodin and T. Schillemans. Oxford: OUP.

Kalen-Sukra, Diane. 2012. "Beating the Corporate Campaign To Privatize Water." *Our Times*. Vol. 31, Issue 1, February-March.

Kanter, R.M. 1994. "Collaborative Advantage: The Art of Alliances." *Harvard Business Review* 72, no. 4 (July-August 1994): 96-108.

Keating, Michael. 1989. "Quo Vadis: Challenges of Public Administration." *Australian Journal of Public Administration* 48: 2, 23-131.

Kernaghan, Kenneth. 2003. "Integrating Values into Public Service: The Values Statement as Centrepiece." *Public Administration Review* Vol. 63, no. 6. November 2003: 711-719.

-- 2006. "Encouraging Rightdoing and Discouraging Wrongdoing: A Public Service Charter and Disclosure Legislation." In *Restoring Accountability - Research Studies Volume 2: The Public Service and Transparency.* Ottawa: Commission of Inquiry into the Sponsorship Program and Advertising Activities.

-- 2007. *A Special Calling: Values, Ethics and Professional Public Service.* Studies and Discoveries Series. Ottawa: Public Service Human Resources Management Agency of Canada.

-- 2009. "Moving Towards Integrated Public Governance: Improving Service Delivery through Community Engagement." *International Review of Administrative Sciences* 75:2: 239-54.

Kettl, Donald. F. 2005. *The Global Public Management Revolution.* Washington, DC: The Brookings Institution.

--2010. "Governance, contract management and public management." In *The New Public Governance*, edited by Stephen P. Osborne, 239-254. New York: Routledge.

Kickert, Walter. 1993. "Complexity, governance and dynamics: conceptual explorations of public network management." In *Modern Governance,* 191-204. London: SAGE Publications Ltd.

Kirkup, James. 2012. "Francis Maude: Civil Service at its smallest since war." *The Telegraph*, February 15, 2012.

Klijn, Erik-Hans. 2005. "Networks and Inter-Organizational Management: Challenging, Steering, Evaluation, and the Role of Public Actors in Public Management." In *The Oxford Handbook of Public Management*, edited by Ewan Ferlie, Laurence E. Lynn, and Christopher Pollitt, 257-81. Oxford: Oxford University Press.

Klijn, Erik-Hans and Joop Koppenjan. 2000. "Public Management and Policy Networks: Foundations of a Network Approach to Governance." *Public Management Review*, 2 (2): 135-58.

Klijn, Erik-Hans and Joop Koppenjan (eds). 1997. *Managing Complex Networks: Strategies for the Public Sector.* London: Sage Publications Ltd.

Kooiman, Jan. 1999. "Socio-Political Governance: Reflections and Design." *Public Management Review*, 1 (1): 67-92.

--2010. "Governance and Governability." In *The New Public Governance: Emerging Perspectives on the Theory and Practice of Public Governance*, edited by Stephen P. Osborne, 72-86. USA and Canada: Routledge.

Koppenjan, Joop and Erik-Hans Klijn. 2004. *Managing Uncertainties in Networks*. London: Routledge.

Kotter, John P. "What Leaders Really Do." *Harvard Business Review*. December 2001, Vol. 79, Issue 11: 85-96.

Lankin, Francis and Munir A. Sheikh. 2012. *Brighter Prospects: Transforming Social Assistance in Ontario: A Report to the Minister of Community and Social Services*. 2012. Toronto: Commission for the Review of Social Assistance in Ontario.

Leadership Centre for Local Government. 2010. *Places, People and Politics: Learning to Do Things Differently Leadership*. London.

Levine, Sol and Paul E. White. 1961. "Exchange as a Conceptual Framework for the Study of Interorganizational Relationships, *Administrative Science Quarterly*, 5 (4): 583-601.

Lindquist, Evert A. 2002. "Culture, control or capacity: meeting contemporary horizontal challenges in public sector management" in M. Edwards and J. Langford (eds.) *New Players, Partners and Processes: a public sector without boundaries?* Canberra and Victoria: National Institute on Governance and UVic Centre for Public Sector Studies.

--2012. "Horizontal Management in Canada Ten Years Later." *Optimum Online: The Journal of Public Sector Management*. September 2012, Vol. 42, Issue 3. Accessed at http://www.optimumonline.ca/print. phtml?e=fjtcgvty&id=422.

Lindquist, Evert, A. and Graham White. 1994. "Ontario Public Service Reform in the 1980's and the 1990's." *Canadian Public Administration*. Summer 1994, Vol. 37 No. 2: 267-301.

Local Government Association. 2012. *Hidden Talents: Supporting the Most Disengaged Young People into Employment Training and Education*. London: Local Government Association.

Lodge, G. and S. Malinowski. 2007. *Innovations in Government: International Perspectives on Civil Service Reform*. London: Institute for Public Policy Research.

Lynn, Laurence E. 2005. "Public Management: A Concise History of the Field." In *The Oxford Handbook of Public Management*, edited by Ewan Ferlie, Laurence E. Lynn, and Christopher Pollitt, 27-50. Oxford: Oxford University Press.

--2006. *Public Management: Old and New*. New York: Routledge.

Mackrael, Kim. 2013. "Justice spending rising sharply as crime rates fall, budget watchdog warns." *Globe & Mail*, March 20. Toronto.

Marsh, David and R. A. W. Rhodes. 1992. *Policy Networks in British Government*. Oxford: Clarendon Press.

Martin, John, 1988. *A Profession of Statecraft: Three Essays on Some Current Issues in the New Zealand Public Service*. Wellington: Institute of Policy Studies.

McCrae, Julian, Jerrett Myers and Katrin Glatzel. 2009. *Undertaking a Fiscal Consolidation: A Guide to Action*. London: Institute for Government.

McKenna, Barry. 2012. "The Hidden Price of Public-Private Partnerships." *Globe and Mail*, October 14.

Metcalfe, Les and Sue Richards. 1991. *Improving Public Management*. London: Sage Publications Ltd.

McLaughlin, Kate, Stephen P. Osborne, and Felie Ewan (eds.). 2002. *New Public Management: Current Trends and Future Prospects*. London: Routledge.

Mendelsohn M., T. Dean, I. Clark, P. Bryant, M. Stabile, J. Hjartarson et al. 2010. *Shifting Gears: Paths to Fiscal Sustainability in Canada*. Toronto: Mowat Centre, University of Toronto.

Ministry of Social Development and Social Innovation (BC). *Employment Program of British Columbia (EPBC)*. Accessed at: Mishra, Ramesh. 1984. *The Welfare State in Crisis: Social Thought and Social Change*. Brighton: Wheatsheaf.

Moore, Mark. 1995. *Creating Public Value - Strategic Management in Government*. Cambridge: Harvard University Press.

Morse, Amyas. 2013. *Integration across Government*. Report by the Comptroller and Auditor General HC 1041 session 2012-13. London: National Audit Office. 13 March.

Nethercote, J.R. 1989. *Public Service Reform: Commonwealth Experience*. Ppaper presented to the Academy of Social Sciences of Australia, 25 February 1989, University House, Australian National University.

Niskanen, William. 1971. *Bureaucracy and Representative Government.* Chicago: Aldine Atherton.

Northcote, Stafford H. and C.E. Trevelyan. 1854. *Report on the Organisation of the Permanent Civil Service.* February 1854. London: Eyre and Spottiswoodie for Her Majesty's Stationary Office. http://www.civilservant.org.uk/northcotetrevelyan.pdf

Nutley, S., S. Morton, T. Jung, and A. Boaz. 2010. "Evidence and Policy in Six European Countries: Diverse Approaches and Common Challenges." *Evidence and Policy,* 6 (2): 131-44.

OECD. 2012. *What Are the Best Policy Instruments for Fiscal Consolidation?* OECD Economics Department Policy Notes, No. 12. April.

OHS Canada. "Alberta Judge Suspends Salary Restraint Act." 24 February 2014. http://www.ohscanada.com/news/alberta-judge-suspends-salary-rrestraint-act/1002928963/

O'Connor, T. H. 2002. *Report of the Walkterton Inquiry, Part 2: A Strategy for Safe Drinking Water.* Toronto: Ontario Ministry of the Attorney General.

Office of the Auditor General, Manitoba. 2003. *A Guide to Policy Development.* Winnipeg: OAG Manitoba.

Oliver Q.C., Hon. Senator Donald. "Adopting the UK 'Accounting Officer' Model in Canada." Paper presented at the Eighth Workshop of Parliamentary Scholars and Parliamentarians at Wroxton College, Oxfordshire, United Kingdom, July 26-27, 2008.

Ontario Hospital Association, Ontario Community Care Access Centres and Ontario Federation of Community Mental Health and Addictions Programs. 2010. *Advice for the Government of Ontario: Ideas and Opportunities for Bending the Health Care Cost Curve.* April.

Ontario Newsroom. 2004. *Canada–Ontario Memorandum of Agreement on Collaboration in the Delivery of Public Service.* Archived Backgrounder. Website of the Office of the Premier of Ontario. Accessed at .

Ontario Public Service Employees' Union. 2014. *Epic Fail: A Short History of Privatization in Ontario.* Toronto: OPSEU.

Osborne, David and Ted Gaebler. 1993. *Reinventing Government.* New York: Penguin Books.

Osborne, Stephen P., ed. 2010. *The New Public Governance: Emerging Perspectives on the Theory and Practice of Public Governance.* Abingdon, Oxfordshire: Routledge.

—2013 "A Services-Influenced Approach to Public Service Innovation?" In *Handbook of Innovation in Public Services,* edited by Stephen P. Osborne and Louise Brown, 60-71. Cheltenham: Edward Elgar.

—2013. *Handbook of Innovation in Public Services.* Cheltenham: Edward Elgar.

Ostrom. V. and E. Ostrom. 1971. "Public Choice: A Different Approach to the Study of Public Administration." *Public Administration Review* 31(2): 203-16.

Ouchi, Willliam. 1979. "Markets, Bureaucracies and Clans." *Administrative Science Quarterly* 25: 129-41.

Page, James, Jonathan Pearson, Briana Jurgeit and Marc Kidson. 2012. *Transforming Whitehall: Leading major change in Whitehall departments.* London: Institute for Government.

Partnership for Public Service. 2011. *Making Smart Cuts: Lessons from the 1990's Budget Front.* Washington, DC: Partnership for Public Service.

Peters, B. Guy. 1998. "Managing Horizontal Government: The Politics of Coordination." *Public Administration* 76:2: 295-311.

—2010. "Meta-Governance and Public Management." In *The New Public Governance: Emerging Perspectives on the Theory and Practice of Public Governance,* edited by Stephen P. Osborne, 36-51. Abingdon, Oxfordshire: Routledge.

Peters, Thomas J. and Robert H. Waterman Jr. 1982. *In Search of Excellence.* New York: Harper & Row.

Pollitt, Christopher. 2008. *Time, Policy, Management: Governing with the Past.* Oxford: Oxford University Press.

—2012. *New Perspectives on Public Services.* Oxford: Oxford University Press.

Pollitt, Christopher and Geert Bouckaert. 2003. "Evaluating Public Management Reforms: An International Perspective." In *Evaluating Public Sector Reforms,* edited by Hellmut Wollman. Aldershot: Edward Elgar.

—2004. *Public Management Reform: A Comparative Analysis.* Oxford: Oxford University Press.

—2011. *Public Management Reform: A Comparative Analysis. New Public Management, Governance and the Neo-Weberian State.* Oxford: The Oxford University Press.

Pressman, Jeffrey L. and Aaron Wildavsky. 1973. *Implementation: How great expectations in Washington are dashed in Oakland or, Why it's Amazing that Federal Programs Work at All.* (3rd Edition). Oakland: University of California Press.

Public Policy Forum. 1998. "Innovation in the Federal Government: The Risk Not Taken." A Discussion Paper Prepared by the Public Policy Forum as a Background Document for a Roundtable Discussion to be held on behalf of the Office of the Auditor General. Ottawa.

--2013. *Ontario's Condominium Act Review: Stage One Findings Report.* Ottawa: Public Policy Forum.

Rainey, Hal G. and Young Han Chun. 2005. "Public and Private Management Compared." In *The Oxford Handbook of Public Management*, edited by Ewan Ferlie, Laurence E. Lynn and Christopher Pollitt, 73-102. Oxford: Oxford University Press.

Rhodes, R. A. W. 1988. *Beyond Westminster and Whitehall: The Sub-Central Governments of Britain.* London: Unwin Hyman.

--1997. *Understanding Governance.* Buckingham: Open University Press.

Roy, Jeffrey and John Langford. 2008. *Integrating Service Delivery Across Levels of Government: Case Studies of Canada and Other Countries.* Washington, DC: IBM Centre for the Business of Government. Accessed at:

Rutter, Jill. 2012. *Opening Up Policy-Making: A Case Study of the National Planning Policy Framework and Other Models of More Open Policy-Making.* London: Institute for Government.

Savas, E.S. 2000. *Privatization and Public-Private Partnerships.* New York: Chatham House.

Savoie, Donald J. 2002. "What is Wrong with the New Public Management." In *Public Management: Critical Perspectives*, edited by Stephen P. Osborne, 263-272. London: Routledge.

Savoie, Donald. 1999. *Governing from the Centre: The Concentration of Power in Canadian Politic.* Toronto: University of Toronto Press.

Scharpf, F.W. 1978. "Interorganizational Policy Studies: Issues, Concepts and Perspectives." In *Interorganizational Policy Making: Limits to Coordination and Central Control*, edited by K. Hanf and F.W. Scharpf, 345-70. London: Sage Publications Ltd.

Schön, Donald A. 1983. *The Reflective Practitioner: How professionals think in action.* Boston: Basic Books.

Scottish Government. 2012. *A Guide to Getting it Right for Every Child.* Accessed at

Seidle, F. Leslie. 1995. *Rethinking the Delivery of Public Services to Citizens.* Ottawa: Institute for Research on Public Policy.

Service Ontario. 2011. "Making it Easier through Joint Service Delivery." Presentation to Tony Dean and Marie Boutilier. January 13, 2011.

Shields, John and B. Mitchell Evans. 1998. *Shrinking the State: Globalization and Public Administration Reform.* Halifax: Fernwood.

Sjowall, Maj, Per Wahloo and Lois Roth. 2008. *Roseanna.* New York: Vintage Books.

Skelcher, Chris. 2005. "Public-Private Partnerships and Hybridity." In *The Oxford Handbook of Public Management,* edited by Ewan Ferlie, Laurence E. Lynn and Christopher Pollitt, 347-370. Oxford: Oxford University Press.

Sousa, Charles. 2013. *A Prosperous and Fair Ontario; 2013 Ontario Budget. Toronto:* Queen's Printer for Ontario.

--2014. *Building Opportunity, Securing Our Future: 2014 Ontario Budget.* Toronto: Queen's Printer for Ontario.

Sparrow, Malcolm. 2000. *The Regulatory Craft: Controlling Risks, Solving Problems and Managing Compliance.* Washington, DC: The Brookings Institution.

--2008. *The Character of Harms: Operational Challenges in Control.* Cambridge: Cambridge University Press.

Sturgess, Gary L. 2012. *Diversity and Contestability in the Public Service Economy.* Australia: NSW Business Chamber.

Swimmer, Gene, and Tim Bartkiw. 2003. "The Future of Public Sector Collective Bargaining in Canada." *Journal of Labour Research* 24, No. 4 (Fall 2003): 579-595.

TD Economics. 2014. "Government Budget Balances and Net Debt as of June 4, 2014." Accessed at http://www.td.com/document/PDF/economics/budgets/gov_budget_20140604.pdf

Task Force on Public Service Values and Ethics. 1996. *A Strong Foundation: Report of the Task Force on Public Service Values and Ethics.* Ottawa: Canadian Centre for Management Development.

Taylor, Frederick. W. 1911. *The Principles of Scientific Management*. New York: Harper.

Terry, Larry D. 1998. "Administrative Leadership, New Managerialism, and the Public Management Movement." *Public Administration Review* 58, no. 3 (May-June 1998): 194-200.

The Canadian Council for Public-Private Partnerships. 2010. *Building Canada's Future: Canadian Attitudes to Public-Private Partnerships 2002-2010*. Toronto Accessed at http://www.pppcouncil.ca/pdf/ppp_survey_2010.pdf

The Conference Board of Canada. 2013. *Canada as a Global Leader: Delivering Value through Public-Private Partnerships at Home and Abroad*. Ottawa: Conference Board.

The Economist. 2012. *Searching for Dave*. Volume 404, Number 8794; July 21-27.

Treasury Board of Canada Secretariat. 2011 (website last modified). *Values and Ethics Code for the Public Sector*. Accessed at http://www.tbs-sct.gc.ca/pol/doc-eng.aspx?section=text&id=25049.

--2012. *Demographic Snapshot of the Federal Public Service*, 2011. Accessed at http://www.tbs-sct.gc.ca/res/stats/demo11-eng.asp#toc01.5.

Tullock, Gordon. 1965. *The Politics of Bureaucracy*. Washington, DC: Public Affairs Press.

U.K. Cabinet Office. 2009. *Power in People's Hands: Learning from the World's Best Public Services*. London: Crown Copyright.

U.K. Department for Education. 2011. *Monitoring and Evaluation of Family Intervention Services and Projects Between February 2007 and March 2011*. Accessed at https://www.gov.uk/government/uploads/system/uploads/attachment_data/file/184031/DFE-RR174.pdf

Ulrich, David, ed. 1998. *Delivering Results: A New Mandate for Human Resource Professionals*. Boston: Harvard Business School Publishing.

Van Wart, Montgomery. 1998. *Changing Public Sector Values*. New York: Garland.

Varney, David. 2006. *A Better Service for Citizens, a Better Deal for the Taxpayer*. HM Treasury: Crown Copyright.

Wood, Dan B. and Richard W. Waterman. 1994. *Bureaucratic Dynamics: The Role of Bureaucracy in a Democracy*. Boulder: Westview.

ENDNOTES

1. Privy Council Office. Deputy Minister Committees. Accessed April 7, 2015.

2. Government of Ontario. Open Government. ;. Accessed April 7, 2015.

3. Government of Alberta. Government of Alberta Mandate. Accessed April 7, 2015.

4. Cabinet Office (UK). Public Service Agreements. UK National Archives website. Last updated 19 January 2009.

5. Cabinet Office (UK). Open Public Services. Accessed April 7, 2015.

6. Department for Communities and Local Government. Support for Families. https://www.gov.uk/government/policies/helping-troubled-families-turn-their-lives-around#issue Last updated 1 May 2014.

7. Department for Communities and Local Government. *Listening to Troubled Families*. Accessed April 7, 2015.

8. Department for Communities and Local Government. *Working with Troubled Families: A guide to evidence and good practice*. Accessed April 7, 2015.

9. Department for Communities and Local Government. *Helping Troubled Families Turn Their Lives Around.* https://www.gov.uk/government/policies/helping-troubled-families-turn-their-lives-around#issue Accessed April 7, 2015.

10. An obvious example was the media's intensive focus on President Obama's first 100 days in office. See Time Magazine; Joe Klein on the President's Impressive Performance Thus Far; April. 23, 2009. http://content.time.com/time/magazine/article/0,9171,1893496,00.html#ixzz2fd64j3up Accessed April 7, 2015.

11. A 2013 government report on progress in implementing the Drummond Report is available at: http://www.fin.gov.on.ca/en/budget/ontariobudgets/2013/ch1c.html#ch1c_5 Accessed April 7, 2015.

12. Government of Ontario Newsroom. *Ontario Government's Plan Is Building Opportunity, Securing Our Future.* News release, November 17, 2004. Accessed April 15, 2015.

13. This chapter is based in part on an essay titled "Is Public Service Delivery Obsolete?" published in the *Literary Review of Canada* in September 2011.

14. Infrastructure Ontario. *AFP Track Record Report.* October 16, 2014. Toronto: The Altus Group.

15. For additional information about Infrastructure Ontario see its website at: . Accessed April 15, 2015.

16. See the website of Social Enterprise Canada at . Accessed April 15, 2015.

17. This chapter relies in part on 2011 research funded by the Ottawa-based Forum of Federations. Marie Boutilier and Tony Dean, *Joint Service Delivery in Federal Countries: A report prepared for the Forum of Federations,* (Ottawa: Forum of Federations, 2012).

18. Robert B. Asselin, Political and Social Affairs Division – Library of Parliament; 18 January 2001 Accessed at . Accessed April 15, 2015.

19. Accenture (2010). *Shared Services Horizons of Value: Leadership Lessons on Accelerating Transformation to High Performance.* http://www.accenture.com/SiteCollectionDocuments/PDF/Accenture-Shared-Services-Horizons-of-Value.pdf#zoom=50. Accessed April 15, 2015.

20. Statistics Canada (2014). *Population by year, by province, by territory.* http://www.statcan.gc.ca/tables-tableaux/sum-som/l01/cst01/demo02a-eng.htm. Last Modified 26 Sept. 2014.

21. For an overview of social enterprises see Elizabeth McIsaac and Carrie Moody, *The Social Enterprise Opportunity for Ontario: Sector Signal Series,* (Toronto: Mowat Centre, 2013).

22. For the current status of Community Budgets and approved pilots see: https://www.gov.uk/government/news/community-budget-pilots-transforming-public-services

23. 2013 TTC Operating Statistics.

24. Correspondence with Andy Byford, August 2013.

25. Interview with Andy Byford, August 2013.

26. This section draws in part from "Accelerating Innovation" an article written by Tony Dean and published in *Canadian Government Executive,* Vol. 17, No. 3 in March 2011. Another version, "Accelerating Innovation in the Public Sector" was co-authored by Tony Dean and Barrett Horne for the Summer 2013 edition of the Yukon Government's *Staff Development Quarterly.*

INDEX

ABOUT THE AUTHOR

Tony Dean teaches public administration at the graduate School of Public Policy and Governance at the University of Toronto. He advises governments in Canada and internationally on public service reform and building capacity for policy-making and delivery. Dean has worked for governments of every political stripe and has observed public services at all levels, including his former role as Cabinet Secretary and head of Ontario's 63,000-member public service. He has led expert reviews on workplace health and safety, pension governance and business and human resource planning for the Government of Canada. Dean has written on public sector leadership and on pathways to fiscal sustainability in Canada. He is a weekly columnist for the Toronto Star's "Queen's Park Briefing". In 2009, Dean was inducted as a member of the Order of Ontario in recognition of his contributions in transforming the Ontario Public Service.

CPSIA information can be obtained
at www.ICGtesting.com
Printed in the USA
BVOW08s0212131217
502605BV00002B/125/P